Bronze Age to Bottle Seals

Glimpses of the Archaeology and History of North Devon

Edited by Terry Green
Published by Museum of Barnstaple & North Devon

Published by
Museum of Barnstaple and North Devon
Copyright ©
North Devon Archaeological Society 2009

ISBN 978 0 9550316 5 6

Cover: Earth penetrating radar survey at
Holworthy Farm Parracombe and a bottle
seal from Torrington.

Back cover: An original document from the
Hartland Archives, dating from 1708 and
leasing a shop to James Nichol, Mariner.

Design by Bruce Aiken
Printed by Russell Press

Contents

Illustrations and maps

Plates

Introduction

The North Devon Archaeological Society is 50 years old this year and to celebrate the Society's respectable age, we have invited a number of interested and well–informed individuals to contribute some of their knowledge to this collection of articles about North Devon. The subjects are as varied as the contributors and because of the Society's brief to promote awareness of the archaeology and history of North Devon they range from the purely archaeological to the wholly historical, the one, we hope, flowing seamlessly into the other. We leave it to readers to 'cherry-pick' the parts they find most interesting.

In landscape terms, most people are probably aware of quite distinct differences between the character of North and South Devon. There are the obvious differences such as the rugged coast of the north as against the more gentle aspect of the south and the fact that the south is more populous than the north. But there is also a division in the minds of the inhabitants, many in the south considering the north of the county remote and almost inaccessible; and in fact until quite recently this might have been almost true, at least for travellers over land. Historically the major routes though Devon ran east to west skirting south of Dartmoor and when 19th century travellers were becoming aware of the meaning of stone settings and barrows and hut circles, their attention was readily drawn to the monuments that litter the Dartmoor landscape and which today make Devon so rich in archaeological sites. Arising out of this circumstance, the interest of regional archaeologists and historians has tended to be directed to the landscapes and settlements of southern Devon, leaving the north relatively neglected. Consequently, and until very recently, the distribution maps of recorded archaeological finds and sites in Devon tended to present the county north of Dartmoor as a blank. North and Northwest Devon appeared to be devoid of anything much, and this apparent absence tended to bolster the old notion (still reflected in many a well intentioned parish history) that before the coming of the stalwart Saxon with his sturdy axe, much of this area was wild and forested; and it also gave rise to the oft repeated remark 'The Romans never came to North Devon'.

Fortunately for those interested in the evolution of the superb North Devon landscape, the picture is now considerably altered. Since W. G. Hoskins kindled interest in the history of the landscape in the 1950s and Lesley Grinsell produced his survey of the archaeology of what he termed 'Greater Exmoor' in the 1960s, new discoveries and a reconsideration of the available evidence have begun to build a picture of a land with a deep and complex history. The broad-based aerial survey carried out over a number of years by Frances Griffith, County Archaeologist , has produced copious evidence of prehistoric settlement throughout Devon; a glance at the distribution maps in the Historical Atlas of South West England (Kain and Ravenhill 1999) provides an illustration of the contribution of the work of Frances Griffith among others, while the recent discoveries of Romano-British iron working sites in the vicinity of Brayford have scotched the notion that North Devon was detached from the Roman world. The development of commercial archaeology through contractors such as Exeter Archaeology and South West Archaeology has had the effect of turning up evidence from the Palaeolithic to the very recent in a quasi-random scatter of locations throughout the county, while the development of the academic discipline of landscape archaeology has shown how the integration of archaeological and historical research in an 'ancient' landscape such as that of North Devon can reveal a complex and deeply interesting story.

So far in this brief introduction we have made much of archaeology. However, this collection is compiled to reflect both the archaeology and the history of the area, and the complementarity of these two approaches to the past is perhaps best illustrated by Chris Preece's piece on bottle seals which, as artefactual evidence dug from the ground, reflect social trends in quite recent historical times. It is self-evident that history and archaeology are complementary, the facts unearthed by one often acting as a corrective to the suppositions derived from the other and both contributing to an account of how we got to where we are today.

In this developing scenario there is too much nascent and on-going work to be fairly represented in such a small volume, and it is admitted straight away that there are some glaring omissions: there is nothing Roman despite what was hinted at above. We have thus opted for a scatter-gun approach, presenting a collection of 18 widely differing papers each of which opens a small window on the changing scene. The contributions are not academic in that they have not been peer-reviewed, but nevertheless they are carefully considered pieces representing a record of growing interest in this region. The 50th birthday of NDAS has offered the reason or excuse to publish this miscellany now. There is no reason however, why we should not look forward to further such collections. Important contributions that immediately come to mind are the Iron Age and Romano-British activities around Brayford and Charles, the recent survey of the 'hillfort' at Knowle near Braunton, documentary and survey work around Hartland and, in the other direction, Parracombe, and the in-depth study of West Yeo Farm near Witheridge. There is much to discover in North Devon and much to communicate to an interested public.

Terry Green

Finally, members of North Devon Archaeological Society would like to express their gratitude to all those who have generously contributed their time and their knowledge to this celebratory publication. Thank you, all of you.

Location map of places mentioned in the text

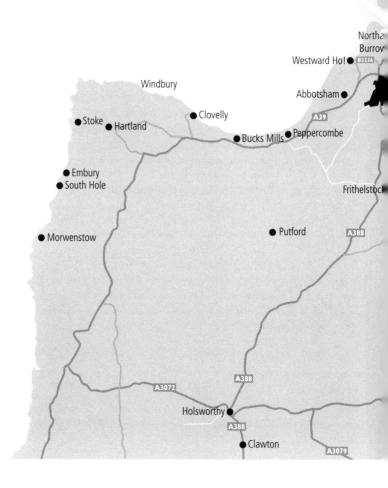

Lundy

Morte Point

Baggy Point

Croyde

Saunton

North
Burrow

Westward Ho! B3236

Windbury

Abbotsham

Stoke Hartland

Clovelly

A39

Bucks Mills Peppercombe

Embury
South Hole

Frithelstock

Morwenstow

Putford

A388

A388

A3072

A388

Holsworthy

A388

Clawton

A3079

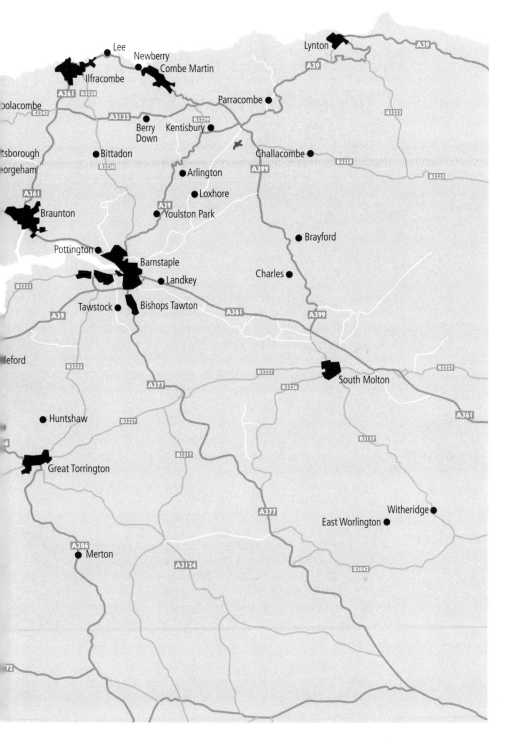

Lee
Newberry
Combe Martin
Lynton
Ilfracombe
A361   B3230
A39
A39
Parracombe
oolacombe
B3343
A3123
B3223
Berry
Down
Kentisbury
B3229
tsborough
Bittadon
Challacombe
B2260
orgeham
B3230
A399
B3223
Arlington
A361
Loxhore
A39
Youlston Park
Braunton
Brayford
Pottington
Barnstaple
Charles
Landkey
B3233
A39
Tawstock
Bishops Tawton
A361
A399
leford
B3232
A377
B3227
B3226
South Molton
B3227
Huntshaw
B3227
A361
B3137
Great Torrington
B3217
Witheridge
East Worlington
A386
A377
Merton
A3124
B3042
72

9

1
Charles Whybrow and Hugh Brooks

The Origin of the North Devon Archaeological Society

In the 6th edition of the Exmoor Review 1964-5, Charles Whybrow wrote the following:

The North Devon Archaeological Society had its origin in an informal group assembled at South Molton in 1958 by Mr H.J.Brooks, Tutor to the Further Education Centre there. During the summer of that year he organised a number of afternoon and evening excursions to interesting sites in North Devon, more especially some of the better known Iron Age hill forts such as Shoulsbury Castle and Mockham Down .... Early in 1959 the group formally constituted itself as the North Devon Archaeological Society, with the usual officers and committee and with headquarters at the South Molton Further Education Centre… (Exmoor Review No.6, 74)

Jonathan Lomas has written this tribute to the Society's first chairman Charles Whybrow

The North Devon Archaeological Society (NDAS) owes its present success to its founder and first chairman, Charles Whybrow (M.A., L.L.B., F.S.A) who died in Somerset, July 1978.

For myself there was a great privilege in knowing him. Both he and his wife were regular attenders at meetings. After his death the membership was well represented at his memorial service at St Peter's Church, Bratton Fleming where he had lived since the early 1950s. He was 76.

Author of 'An Antiquary's Exmoor' and a contributor to the Transactions of the Devonshire Association, he was Vice-President of the Exmoor Society.

Charles Whybrow was educated at Berkhamstead School, Hertfordshire and Christ's College, Cambridge. He was called to the Bar (a non-practicing barrister) and during a colonial civil service career with the Education Department in what was then Tanganyika was headmaster of the school at Malangali. Later he became Provincial Education officer of Lake Province, Lake Victoria. During World War II he was an officer in the King's African Rifles.

On his retirement to North Devon he became Governor of West Buckland School, a member of Bratton Fleming Parish Council, Chairman of St Peter's Parochial Church Council and both a reader and a benefactor of the church, donating a 'Good News' bible for the lectern.

His contributions to the Exmoor Review were numerous. He also wrote an unpublished history of Bratton Fleming. In 1959, under the leadership of Charles Whybrow and Hugh Brooks, tutor at the Further Education Centre in South Molton, the North Devon Archaeological Society was formally constituted and Charles Whybrow became its first chairman. He always attended NDAS field meetings, arriving in his familiar maroon Wolseley 1500 where his wife would remain seated throughout the proceedings, usually reading the newspaper. His entertaining manner and dry wit were one of his memorable and endearing qualities that I recall, but woe betide anyone who dared to chatter during any of his talks. He conducted us on tours of Cadbury Castle in Somerset, Chapman Barrows above Parracombe and the earthworks above Hillsford Bridge on the East Lyn River. Roughtor near Camelford was a favourite with him as well as the Cheesewring on Bodmin Moor. On one occasion we even ventured across the railway viaduct at Filleigh on a Sunday when no trains were scheduled, as none ever ran on this day by Act of Parliament.

The passing of Charles Whybrow was a great loss to the North Devon Archaeological Society at a time when it was building its strength in membership and becoming a well respected and recognised society within the South West.

Plate 1.1
Hugh Brooks explaining a point to the North Molton Local History Class in the 1950s. (Western Morning News)

2

The North Devon Athenaeum 1880 to 2008

Margaret Reed

The Athenaeum in Barnstaple was founded by William Frederick Rock [1802-1890], a Barnstaple man who spent almost his entire adult life in London, but never forgot the town of his birth or the physical and intellectual needs of its inhabitants.

The list of his benefactions to Barnstaple is impressive – in 1845 he established a free library in the High Street. This was followed in the 1870s by Rock Park and in the 1880s he established a convalescent home at Mortehoe for the use of poor people on being discharged from the North Devon Infirmary.

His final venture was the purchase of a new building on The Square, owned by a former Mayor, William Thorne, which William fitted out, filled with books and generously endowed. This was The North Devon Athenaeum, opened on 22nd August 1888, specifically for the free access of all – as it is to this day – administered by The Rock Trustees and a Board of Directors.

The Athenaeum occupied this building until 1988 when the Devon County Council, which leased the ground floor for the Barnstaple Library, moved the library to its new home in Tuly Street. The Athenaeum moved together with the library, leasing its own suite of rooms on the second floor while retaining its separate identity and staff. Meanwhile, the building on The Square was sold to the North Devon District Council for use as The Museum of Barnstaple and North Devon.

After 120 years the North Devon Athenaeum still carries out the wishes of its founder in welcoming all comers to study its books and archives free of charge. His wish was that there should be no 'periodical trash' provided, as it should be a place for study rather than a lounge. In particular, he did not want it to be used as a place where ladies of the town interviewed prospective servants. His wishes in this last respect are strictly observed.

The Trustees and Directors are very grateful to past and present benefactors who have enabled this privately endowed free library to remain open to the people of Barnstaple and beyond, as its founder intended.

3

Archaeology in the North Devon Journal 1824-74

Peter Christie

In the following the numbers in brackets refer to the editions of the Journal and other sources listed at the end.

The *North Devon Journal* was first published on July 1 1824 under the editorship of John Avery.(1) Over the first 50 years of the paper's history he and his successors printed a selection of what might be termed archaeological items which this article will examine.

The first of these does not appear until May 1830 when a discovery at Bideford was announced (2). The item reads in its entirety 'On Thursday last, a Roman Coin was found on the estate of W.S.Tyeth, Esq. of the reign of the Emperor A.Vitellius Germanicus, in a very fine state of presentation, being now 1751 years old.' No more direct references follow until June 1833 when a skeleton was unearthed at Rumsam in Barnstaple (3). Identified as a female aged about 18, it was thought to be from a gipsy group who had camped there some 30 years previously. Two years later some coffins were revealed five feet deep on the site of a new house at 'the higher end' of Bear Street which were suggested to belong to 'plague victims' (4). Further similar finds came from the same area in 1848 and again were identified as plague victims (5). Another 'out-of-place' skeleton turned up at Joy Street, Barnstaple in 1860 and in the same year at Ashford.(6)

In May 1856 the *Journal* carried a long description of the discovery of the 'giant' skeletons on Lundy supposed to measure, in one case, eight feet five inches (7). A modern article has detailed these finds (8). Eight years later in November 1864 the *Journal* reported that a skeleton had been brought to light during work on constructing a new embankment at Pottington just outside of Barnstaple (9). A local antiquary wrote a paper on this which he presented to the Barnstaple Literary and Scientific Institution averring that the remains which included a skull showing evidence 'of a severe blow' were of 'a sailor in a Scandinavian war galley' (10). I assume this was inspired guesswork rather than a well thought out supposition based on evidence.

Future archaeologists uncovering empty graves in North Devon might like to bear in mind that North Devon was subject to the attentions of grave robbers. In April 1829, for example, a man from Carmarthen turned up at a meeting of the directors of the North Devon Infirmary in Barnstaple offering to obtain bodies for the surgeons (11)!

With intriguing timing, just 2 weeks before the report of the Lundy 'giants' appeared, the *Journal* carried a note that the Barnstaple Literary and Scientific Institute had established an 'Archaiologic Club' (12). Its first meeting heard a paper on 'Barnstaple as a fortress' which dealt with the Civil War fortifications at Ebberly Place. No other meetings are reported, so possibly this first incarnation of the North Devon Archaeological Society did not take off?

Skeletons were not the only thing being reported on by the *Journal*. In February 1854 a long simmering dispute over the enclosure of the Commons at Lynton came to the boil. One of the disputants, a Mr.Bailey, published correspondence on the subject between him and Messrs.Roe and Riccard in the form of a pamphlet which the *Journal* quoted from extensively (13). In this he strenuously defended himself against charges that he was 'seeking to destroy the romantic and beautiful scenery of the Valley of the Rocks'. Indeed, he attacked 'those who have misused it for the last fifty years', citing as one example 'the removal of the immense Druidical stones and circles, and the rocks which formed its peculiar and striking interest and beauty, for the purpose of selling them for gate posts.' These must be the same stones Polwhele refers to in his History of Devonshire and which are briefly touched on by J.R.Chanter in his 1867 paper 'The Early History and Aborigines of North Devon' (14).

In 1857 the *Journal* covered the finding of a coin dating from the reigns of Elizabeth/James I which had been found hidden in a roof at Hartland (15). Thomas Chope of Farford had got possession of it, though where it is today is unknown. That coin finds were rare or unreported is evident, as over the next 17 years only one other, from Barnstaple in 1866 (of Henry VIII), has been noted (16).

In 1858 five cannons were uncovered at low tide off Northam Burrows.(17) Being some seven feet long, only two were saved in the narrow time window available and these ended up on display at Glenburnie House. They were assumed to be from HMS *Weazel*, a Royal Navy brig which had sunk in Bideford Bay in 1799.

Eight years after this discovery the *Journal* published the exciting news that two holidaying geologists had discovered 'curious antiquarian specimens of instruments' in the clay on Westward Ho! beach.(18) Indeed, so exciting were the finds that the formation of a museum to display them was mooted. A letter printed just afterwards, however, deemed them to be relatively modern.(19) Signed 'A Local Antiquarian' the writer noted 'I have since heard those relics spoken of as "An Indian tomahawk" and as a portion of ancient armour' but he dismissed them saying 'One is an iron ring belonging to a ship's anchor, or chain; whilst the "tomahawk" is simply a large hammer, singularly incrusted by the action of salt water, with a coating of sand and small pebbles' – and he reckoned they came from a fairly recent shipwreck.

This year of 1866 was something of a 'red letter' one for local archaeology as in October Mr.Spence Bates gave a talk to the Plymouth Institution on the flint tools of North Devon which he reckoned were 'abundant'(20). The report of this in the *Journal* was accompanied by a letter from Nicholas Whitley of Penarth who strongly challenged Bence's assertion that 'the flakes are arrow heads, the result of human labour' (21). He went on, 'It fell my lot, some four years back, to discover these Croyde flakes' which he reckoned were 'naturally formed' He supported this argument with six points, including the fact that some were so small they 'would not kill a mouse' – and that others had been found 'around the dreary Dozmare Pool [Dartmoor], where men from choice would never locate themselves.'

A week later, the well-known North Devon geologist Townshend M.Hall wrote in reply from Pilton Parsonage (22). He noted that he had described the Croyde flints and some associated 'sunbaked and rudely fashioned' pottery in a paper read to the Society of Antiquaries in December 1864. In a closely reasoned argument he pointed out that most students of such flints accepted their human origin, and ended his letter with a modern sounding request; 'Should…any of the intelligent members of the Farmers' Clubs, at Barnstaple or Bideford, ever find (either in ploughing their land or in making excavations for drains etc) long pieces of flint, which look pointed, they would do me a favour by informing me of the circumstance, so that I might be able to make an examination of the locality.' Whitley returned to the discussion the next week both attacking Hall and again reckoning the 'flints' were natural (23). This stimulated both Hall and a Charles Johnston to reply, both of whom rejected Whitley's hypothesis (24.)

In December 1866 Spence Bates gave his talk to the Exeter Naturalists' Club and this was reported at length in the *Journal* (25). Bates argued that the flints were actually made by 'Belgic Gauls' but Whitley, who was present, once more refuted any human involvement which led to Sir James Bowring saying 'He was astonished at the courage of Mr.Whitley in denying the human origin of those weapons.' Bates went on to publish an article entitled 'An attempt to approximate the date of the flint flakes of Devon and Cornwall' in the *Popular Science Review*, which included two pages of engravings of the flints in question (26.)

This flurry of interest was followed up by H.S.Ellis of Exeter in a paper to the 1867 meeting of the British Association in Aberdeen on 'Mammalian Remains from the Submerged Forest in Barnstaple Bay, Devonshire' which had been found in proximity to flint tools (27). Intriguingly the paper referred to 'a tradition in North Devon, that the oak trees used for the roof and seats of the Church of Braunton grew in a forest which formerly occupied the site of the Burrows, and that the trees, when felled, were drawn to the church by red deer.' This talk was followed up by a lecture to the Exeter Athenaeum by Mr.Pengelly on 'The Submerged Forests of Devonshire' which discussed the Westward Ho! example in detail (28).

This plentiful coverage of archaeology seems to have generated interest in the subject if we are to judge from two long articles which appeared in July 1867 (29). Both are concerned with the 'Opening of an Ancient British Barrow', the first at Putford, the second at Huntshaw. The latter was written up in the *Transactions of the Devonshire Association* and the former has been covered by myself (30). Needless to say, both of the accounts in the *Journal* are redolent of a previous age.

At Putford the Reverend May had supervised the cutting of a 'convenient gallery two feet wide' north-south through the entire tumulus. Unfortunately for the clergyman and 'a numerous party of scientific gentlemen' who attended the opening 'it soon became evident that industrious searchers had certainly been there' before them. Small 'loaf' shaped baked clay articles were found – the feeling being that these were 'some kind of votive offering'. The 'dig' was followed by 'a dinner, al fresco, under a shaded bank along which the carriage cushions had been comfortably arranged.' The Huntshaw excavation, which saw two 'barrows' opened in as many hours, found little but 'numerous portions of well-carbonized wood', though the newspaper report does give a paragraph to describing different soil layers noticed during the operations – an early example of stratigraphic evidence.

Just above the account of the Huntshaw expedition is the first appearance of 'Our Antiquarian Corner' wherein 'local historic and archaeological' notes were invited. Run by 'Marland' (the pen name of J.R.Powell) this ran for many years, although the emphasis soon came to centre on the genealogy of manorial lords and gentry.

In December 1868 the *Journal* published a letter from Christopher Cooke of London regarding the discovery of a 'medieval' gold and diamond ring at Frithelstock. Apparently the 'emblems' on it 'are typical of the Holy Trinity, our Saviour, Virgin Mary, and St. Thomas a Becket.' (31). A week later the ring's owner Charles Spence wrote in, his letter being headed 'Frithelstock Priory' (32). He recounted its rather uncertain provenance: 'I bought it some years ago of Mr. Dungey, linen draper, of Bedford Street, Plymouth, and was informed that it had been discovered among the ruins of the Priory together with some coins. Beyond that I know nothing of its antecedents.'

It was to be another three years before the *Journal* returned to archaeological topics. In 1871 the massive new 'Ilfracombe Hotel' was in course of construction in that town when a 'Remarkable discovery' was made at a depth of fourteen feet (33). One of the labourers, John Blackford, found a rounded stone some six inches by five inches with 'hole of half an inch width' drilled through the centre. Those who viewed it considered it a fishing net weight. Only 4 months later Ilfracombe threw up another discovery when stone was being quarried on Lantern Hill (34). Human bones were exposed and the report noted, 'The piece of table land immediately below the old chapel, at the summit of the hill, was formerly used, it is said, as a burial ground, and it was in this spot these bones were disturbed.'

The final archaeological report published up to July 1874 came from Abbotsham (35). A visitor from Exeter, Mr. Glendinning, literally stumbled over a cache of some 50 Roman coins that had been exposed in the root of a tree. Amongst them were sestertii of Diocletian and Severus Alexander. The *Journal* noted that the finder 'says he shall regard [them] as a very gratifying souvenir of his visit to the locality.'

As I said at the beginning of this article, the *Journal* did publish archaeological items from almost its inception and should, I believe, be regarded as a valuable source of such material. I hope this review has proved my assertion.

References

1   The files are held in the North Devon Athenaeum, Tuly Street, Barnstaple
2   North Devon Journal (NDJ) 6.5.1830
3   NDJ 20.6.1833 4c
4   NDJ 9.7.1835 4d
5   NDJ 3.2.1848 3a
6   NDJ 23.2.1860 4f + 19.7.1860 5a
7   NDJ 15.5.1856 5c
8   Transactions of the Devonshire Association (TDA) 1997. K.Gardner &
    M.Ternstrom 'The Giants Graves'
9   NDJ 24.11.1864 5d
10 NDJ 30.3.1865 5d
11 NDJ 2.4.1829 4a + TDA 1996 P.Christie 'Folklore in North Devon'
12 NDJ 1.5.1856 5d-e
13 NDJ 16.2.1854 8c-d
14 Richard Polwhele 'The History of Devonshire' 1797 Vol.1 p.140 + TDA 1867
    J.R.Chanter 'The Early History and Aborigines of North Devon'
15 NDJ 25.6.1857 8a
16 NDJ 19.4.1866 5c
17 NDJ 25.3.1858 5b & 8e + 8.4.1858 8a
18 NDJ 24.4.1866 2d-e
19 NDJ 26.4.1866 2d
20 NDJ 18.10.1866 6d-e
21 NDJ 18.10.1866 8e-f
22 NDJ 25.10.1866 5e-f
23 NDJ 1.11.1866 8e-f
24 NDJ 8.11.1866 8b-c
25 NDJ 13.12.1866 6a
26 NDJ 25.4.1867 6a
27 NDJ 12.9.1867 5d
28 NDJ 26.3.1868 6b
29 NDJ 4.7.1867 8b-c + 18.7.1867 8a-b
30 TDA 1867 H.Fowler 'On the opening of an ancient British barrow at
    Huntshaw' + P.Christie 'Putford Burial Mound 1867' NDJ 21.7.1988
31 NDJ 3.12.1868 5e
32 NDJ 10.12.1868 6c
33 NDJ 16.2.1871 8e
34 NDJ 22.6.1871 5e
35 NDJ 12.3.1874 8b

4

North Devon Areas of Outstanding Natural Beauty:
Historic Landscape

Linda Blanchard

The North Devon Coastal area was designated as an Area of Outstanding Natural Beauty (AONB) in 1959 and in 2000 the Countryside and Rights of Way Act confirmed AONB landscapes as being of equivalent status to that of a National Park. In 2004 the North Devon AONB Partnership was created to concentrate on the area and its small staff unit co-ordinates the delivery of a management plan to secure a sustainable future for our coast.

One role of the Partnership is to understand and define qualities which contribute to the character of the AONB. It is the area's distinctiveness that attracts visitors and contributes to our enjoyment, health and local economy. In order to keep the AONB beautiful whilst meeting the needs of those who depend on it for their homes and livelihood, two tools have been developed in Devon:

*• **Landscape Characterisation:** This involves mapping the geology, soils, habitats, land form, land use present and past to form units of similar character and management needs.*
*• **Historic Landscape Characterisation:**. Using historic maps and overlays we can start to understand how the landscape was used in the past.*

A third piece of work has been undertaken by Exeter Archaeology which listed all recorded historic environment data for the North Devon AONB. This article pulls together the conclusions of this work to explore the relationship between North Devon's landscape and its past historic use. The codes in bold refer to Devon Landscape Character types present in the AONB.

The most significant influence on the AONB's landscape has been the sea as it provides food, ease of transport and a means of defence. *Inter-tidal sand (LCT 4E)* is found around the Taw Torridge estuary mouth and at the popular tourist beaches. Subjected to the extreme tides of the Bristol Channel, at first glance this zone would appear to be devoid of any historic interest. However at Westward Ho! there is evidence of very early occupation including a submerged forest, shell midden of Mesolithic times, possible Neolithic timber stakes which may have marked an ancient trackway, and possibly Romano-British timber fish traps.

Nearby the *unsettled Marine Levels (LCT4B)* with their scant low salt marsh and mudflats show only a fish trap near Crow Point.

Moving inland, North Devon exhibits *coastal dunes (LCT4F)* at Northam, Braunton, Croyde, and Woolacombe. At Braunton Burrows the vast dune system (designated for its wildlife as the core of the North Devon UNESCO Biosphere Reserve) may well conceal remains from almost any period: 18th century maps, for example, indicate a lost chapel site. The use of the Burrows for rabbit warrens was important in the 18th century. However, it is the internationally important Second World War evidence (Plate 4.1) which really marks the historic character of this landscape. As the Allies prepared to invade Normandy, the coastline from the mouth of the Taw to Morte Point was appropriated by the US Army and the remains of training structures are still present, the most notable being the five replica landing craft in Braunton Burrows.

Cliff (LCT 5) also includes narrow shingle beaches and rocky foreshore found along the majority of the AONB coast. At Hartland Quay, immense chunks of rusting

Plate 4.1
Concrete replica
landing-craft near
Crow Point.
(photo: Explore
Braunton Project
and Christie Estates)

19

ironwork from one of around 130 shipwrecks on this dangerous coast bring home the scale of these past disasters and at Rapparee (Ilfracombe) and Croyde, human remains, believed to be of drowned sailors, have been found in the cliff edge.

The cliff edge has always been a major line of defence with the earliest remains being the dramatic Iron Age cliff castles and hillforts. Hillsborough (Plate 4.2) is the largest but others include Newberry, Peppercombe, Embury and Windbury. More recent remains include a Victorian gun battery at Hillsborough, World War II radar stations at Hartland and Northam, and transmitter masts along the coast.

Lime took the place of sand as the main agricultural aid from the 16th century and limekilns are commonplace in the area; those at Bucks Mills (Plate 4.3) are especially fine. Some have the remains of channels carved out to give better access by ship with evocative names such as the Peppercombe Lear and Blackpit at Lee. At Greencliff (Abbotsham) the kiln took advantage of a local outcrop of culm as fuel.

The villages of Clovelly and Bucks Mills are built into the steep cliff and together with Hartland Quay have harbours which, from the 16th century, sheltered herring fishing fleets, an important industry until the early 20th Century.

The rocky foreshore and cliffs are also home to some more unlikely features associated with the rise of tourism: the famous tunnels with sea water bathing pools cut into the foreshore at Ilfracombe are a fine example.

Open coastal plateau (LCT1B) describes the high land behind the beaches and cliffs, mainly in Torridge, where finds of flint and chert tools (Baggy Point, Hartland, and Abbotsham) suggest Mesolithic and Neolithic occupation. Bronze Age barrows are found on Berry Down, and elsewhere standing stones can also be found. The high ground to the south of Ilfracombe is a good example where there is a hillslope enclosure at North Hill Cleave, Bittadon.

Plate 4.2
View of the cliff castle or promontory fort at Hillsborough, Ilfracombe. (photo Neville Stannikk)

Hartland is the only large settlement on high land within the AONB and is more akin to villages found in Cornwall. Nearby names such as Berry, Blegberry, Tosberry and Titchberry may indicate prehistoric enclosed settlements. Hartland became a borough in the late 13th century and the high tower of the church of St Nectan at Stoke (Plate 4.4) and the nearby folly (perhaps a warrener's tower dating to the 16th or 17th century) are important landmarks. There are strong early Christian associations (St Nectan and others), and a collegiate chapel was founded at Stoke in the 11th century to be succeeded in the 12th century by an Augustinian monastery.

The plateau is essentially a farmed landscape with enclosed field systems. Some fields, especially on the higher land, were clearly marked out anew by surveyors in the 18th and 19th centuries. Others are based on the medieval strip field system with some showing their characteristic curving boundaries, others having resulted from the amalgamation of strips in late or post-medieval times.

Coastal Scarp slopes and combes (LCT2B) are scored deep into the Hartland plateau. These represented the most intensively settled areas with many farmsteads and hamlets originating during the medieval period. They nestle within an intimate landscape still dominated by enclosed medieval field systems. However, centuries of use have resulted in an intricate pattern with orchards, woodlands, formal gardens at Hartland Abbey, water-meadows, and deerparks upstream.

Settled Coastal Combes (LCT2F) are found from Lee to Combe Martin. Combe Martin with its comparative mineral wealth contains the main concentration of industrial archaeological evidence within the AONB. Here there are significant

Plate 4.3
Lime-kilns at Buck's Mills.
(photo Neville Stannikk)

Plate 4.4
St Nectan's Church
Stoke, Hartland.
(photo Stephen
Hobbs)

remains relating to silver and lead mines which were worked at intervals from the medieval period through to the late 19th century. There is also a concentration of limekilns around the quarries south of the town. The other settled combes are more pastoral, for example Berrynarbor, a traditional farming village characterised by cob and thatch.

The Steep Open Slopes (LCT2G) at Woolacombe have been substantially overlaid by settlement which is strongly Edwardian in character and largely developed following the local arrival of the railway in 1874.

The lower rolling farmland (LCT3B) at Croyde and Saunton has a strong remnant medieval form. Croyde especially has retained its medieval village core, its character enhanced by several groups of fossilised strip fields. Nearby, Saunton has surviving medieval lynchets but takes much of its character from the strong architectural statements of the 1930s Saunton Sands Hotel and other 20th century tourist facilities. Nearby the listed Saunton Court also has gardens designed by Lutyens.

Farmed lowland moorland (LCT1F) is rare within the AONB and is more commonly known as Culm Grasslands. It is found primarily at Bursdon and Welsford Moors where we find extensive barrow cemeteries, but is otherwise largely unenclosed pasture. Situated within more enclosed farmland is Clovelly Dykes which covers an area of 8 hectares and is a classic example of a 'south western' hillfort with widely spaced earthwork defences.

The *unsettled farm valley floor (LCT 4A)* of Braunton Marsh and Great Field is a rich agricultural land sheltered from the weather by Braunton Burrows. Not at present part of the designated AONB, they are amongst the most important historic landscapes in the region and we hope ultimately that they will receive much needed protection by gaining AONB status in the future.

The Great Field, although much eroded, is one of the best surviving medieval field systems in the country and still farmed in strips separated by low earthen baulks and marked by bond-stones. Braunton and Horsey Marshes were carved out of the estuary by entrepreneurs in the 19th century and are packed with historic engineering works and field barns.

Although scant, the information and evidence we have on historic environment in the AONB gives us a glimpse of the area's substantial and fascinating resources and the gaps in our knowledge indicate a lack of research. The majority of recent field research in Hartland, the Estuary, and in Combe Martin, has been entirely as a result of voluntary effort and a major challenge for the next few years is to ensure that there is at least an equivalent level of effort from those who have the responsibility. To understand and preserve our historic environment is key.

Notes

The North Devon AONB Landscape Character types are more fully explained in our draft management plan The North Devon Coast downloadable from www.northdevoncoast.org.uk. A topic paper on the Historic Environment of the AONB can be found on the same site. The Devon Historic Landscape Characterisation can be viewed on the County Council website www.devon.gov.uk

5

A Bronze Age Settlement at Holworthy Farm, Parracombe

Terry Green

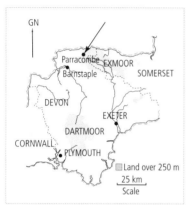

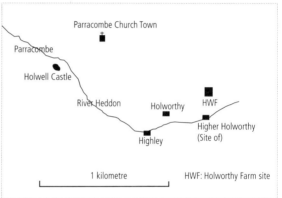

Fig. 5.1
Location of the
Holworthy Farm
(HWF) site.

The initial aim of the North Devon Archaeological Society's Parracombe Project was to emulate – as far as might be possible for a local society – the University of Bristol's Shapwick Project. This comprehensive study of a Somerset village and parish is now completed and represents a model for settlement based landscape projects in general. To date progress with the Parracombe Project has been uneven, but enough archaeological and historical information has been accumulated to lay the basis of a more co-ordinated study in the future. However, within the context of the project, the study of Holworthy Farm is perhaps nearest to being rounded off and within that framework the excavation of a hillslope enclosure on the farm's land represents a successfully completed and regionally important piece of work, representing, to date, the only excavation of a prehistoric settlement on Exmoor.

Holworthy Farm lies beside the headwaters of the River Heddon (See Location maps, Fig. 5.1) which flows into the Bristol Channel at Heddon's Mouth. The earliest documentary mention of Holworthy dates from 1213, but a settlement will have existed here before that date. The *worthy* element in the name Holworthy ('enclosure in the hollow') may betray a pre-Conquest origin and it is possible that the site of the present farm buildings is successor to an earlier settlement farther up the valley, perhaps

the now abandoned Higher Holworthy whose location is somewhat more characteristic of Saxon farmsteads in Devon. Like its neighbours Highley and Twineford, Holworthy sits below the ridge between Parracombe and Challacombe which is marked by the Bronze Age barrow cemetery known as Chapman Barrows. These round barrows together with other burial mounds in the vicinity and the evidence of early settlements on South Common and on west-facing ground to the east, suggest a Bronze Age population exploiting the fertile, sheltered land of Parracombe.

The remains of an enclosure on the hillside above Higher Holworthy (Plate 5.1) at 340m above OD were first noted in recent times through an aerial survey of 1979, subsequent to which it was visited by Hazel Eardley-Wilmot and was recorded in the Sites and Monuments Register. The site is only visible in low light conditions when the very slight elevation of the surrounding bank can be discerned as a shadow mark defining an ovoid enclosure some 40m x 30m. This has been identified as a 'hillslope enclosure', a regional catch-all term for (presumed) prehistoric enclosures – circular, ovoid or rectilinear – on hillslopes. These are comparable to the rounds of Cornwall and similar enclosed settlements throughout the highland zone of western Britain.

We were aware that in Devon and Exmoor only one such site had ever been investigated by excavation, namely a hillslope enclosure at Rudge near Morchard Bishop (Todd 1998). This turned out to be Romano-British in date. Apart from this one instance, these sites remained largely a mystery, and there was great interest in learning more about them. As the Holworthy site was not scheduled and as we had access to the necessary skills, our study of Holworthy Farm presented the opportunity to investigate another example.

In July 2002, having received all the necessary permissions, we first set out to ascertain the state of preservation of the monument. Removing a 10m x 1.5m strip of turf from the least visible part of the enclosure, we found immediately beneath the turf a spread of sandstone rubble within which was a somewhat denser band where the enclosure bank should have been. From this we suspected and it was later

25

confirmed, that the site was enclosed by a bank of piled stone which, over the centuries, had been spread by ploughing. There was no outer ditch, as might have been supposed, which immediately set the site apart from the 'classic' banked and ditched settlements of the Iron Age. In fact, in the method of enclosure this suggested comparison with Bronze Age settlements such as Grimspound and Shaugh Moor on Dartmoor. This initial brief excavation provided no dating evidence apart from a few flints which at this stage told us nothing.

In July 2003 we returned to the site, having commissioned a gradiometer survey which suggested features for investigation. This time we set out two long trenches in an L-formation in the interior of the enclosure in the area where a previous English Heritage topographic survey (see Riley and Wilson-North 2001, 72) had suggested there might be a building platform. As before, large quantities of sandstone rubble were found beneath the turf. Near the point where our two trenches formed a right angle, a sharp-eyed excavator noted sherds of pottery, which turned out to be part of a vessel, the base and lower body of which were intact and standing upright, having apparently been protected by the spread of rubble. On examination by Henrietta Quinnell (University of Exeter), this turned out to be a Middle Bronze Age vessel in the Trevisker style, giving us our first indication of a date for the enclosure. In addition we found in the angle of the two trenches a cut feature, a short length of shallow gully full of charcoal and topped off with large stones. These two finds together prompted further, more extensive excavation in the following two years.

In summer 2004 and 2005 around 50% of the interior of the enclosure was excavated (Fig. 5.2). The short length of gully uncovered in 2003 turned out to be part of a long shallow trench which snaked its way across some 12 metres of the northern,

Fig. 5.2:
The extent of excavation within the enclosure.

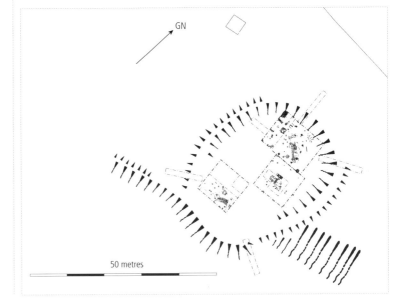

GN

50 metres

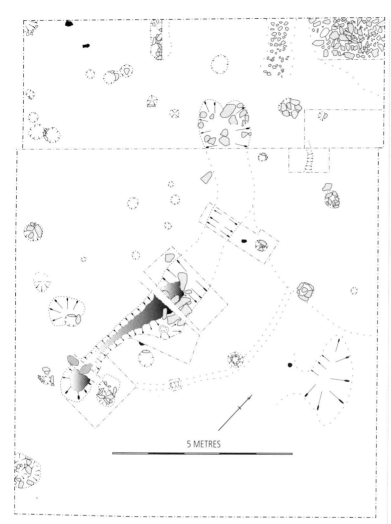

Fig. 5.3
Excavated area
within the northern
part of the enclosure
with the circle of
large post-holes,
including 'doubles'
and the ash-filled
gulley running
through it.

upslope part of the site. Several metres of the gully were filled with charcoal or charcoal impregnated silts, and from this and other deposits of charcoal, samples were sorted out for radiocarbon dating. The results of this confirmed that the enclosure had originated in the Middle Bronze Age around 1500 BC and that occupation had continued until around 1100 BC. Closely associated with the gully was a ring of large post-holes which strongly suggested a roundhouse. Curiously, the long, sinuous gully seemed to enter the roundhouse through what might have been a porch and to traverse its centre (Fig. 5.3). This would have made for awkward living, though it was not clear that these two major features were contemporary within the 400 years of occupation. Numerous other post-holes in this part of the site failed to suggest any pattern. Towards the southern end of the enclosure a 10x5 metre excavation revealed a second charcoal filled gully along the edge of which were large post-holes and in the base of which was a deposit of pottery sherds which were identifiable as Trevisker ware. Nearby was a scatter of post-holes which were characteristically D-shaped or wedge-shaped in plan, suggesting the use of split logs. Here also were groups of small stake-holes which suggested the location of hurdles or wattle structures. On the periphery of the excavated area, further glimpses of the enclosure boundary confirmed its construction with piled stone. Excavation in the centre of the enclosure revealed what might have been a pit which had been short-lived and rapidly back-filled. A radio-carbon determination obtained from charcoal recovered from the upper fill gave the earliest date on the site, around 1700 BC, indicating Bronze Age activity here before the creation of the enclosure.

Pottery recovered from the excavation amounted to 230 sherds including the two major deposits mentioned above. Apart from six small sherds of an Iron Age ware found in the hillwash in the lower part of the site (see below), the ceramic assemblage consistently represented Middle Bronze Age Trevisker ware and was comparable in style and decoration to pottery from Trethellen Farm, North Cornwall (Nowakowski 1991), a site of similar date. The fabric was locally made, the clays possibly sourced from coastal glacial deposits and was comparable with materials from Doniford, near Williton, Somerset, the only other excavated Middle Bronze Age site of the Exmoor area. Other ceramic objects included three fragments of baked clay representing what are usually thought to be loomweights.

The relative chronology of the excavated features presented problems which are still not fully resolved. Outstanding among the difficulties was the discovery of a pair of adjacent post-holes − part of the post-ring - which produced vastly different radio-carbon dates, one firmly Middle Bronze Age, the other just as firmly Middle Iron Age, ie. about 1000 years younger. Iron Age dates were also obtained from two other post-holes within the post-ring, but could not with confidence be regarded as dating the features themselves, since the small quantities of charred organic matter could have been introduced by worm action. All together 15 radiocarbon determinations were obtained, 11 of which indicated Middle Bronze Age activity. Three pointed to a period of the Iron Age between 370 and 150 BC, and one suggested the later Bronze Age, around 900 BC. Since these later dates all came from post-holes of the post-ring, the simplest conclusion would be that the post-ring/roundhouse was of Iron Age date suggesting re-occupation of the enclosure in this later period, a possibility reinforced by the presence of a small quantity of Iron Age pottery in the hillwash in the lower part of the site. However, two of the major post-holes produced firm Middle Bronze Age dates. These holes were 'stuffed' with oak charcoal, excluding any possibility of worm action and thus more conclusively dating them than did the very small amounts of Iron Age charcoal or charred grain that dated the others. In addition, a number of the post-holes of the post-ring had received a final treatment − removal of the post and blocking of the hole with a stone − which in Cornwall had been seen as characteristic of Bronze Age behaviour (see below). The conclusion (for the moment at least) is therefore that the post-ring is of Middle Bronze Age date. The one firmly dated Iron Age post-hole possibly belongs to a structure of which we have seen only this single element and which coincidentally was made adjacent to a much older hole, of which the Iron Age people would have had no knowledge.

However, if the post-ring in fact represented a Bronze Age roundhouse – or at least a circular structure – then what was the long gully with its content of fire ash doing running through the middle of it? As suggested above, the two features were quite possibly not contemporary, but the radiocarbon dates that we have do not help us to separate them in time. It may be, of course, that they actually belong together and are involved in some activity that we do not understand.

The nature of this activity is perhaps hinted at by a find associated with the long gully. Found lying face down beside the southern end of the gully was a small ovoid saddle quern (Plate 5.2). Shaped from a block of gritty sandstone, this small quern is comparable to similar finds on Bronze Age sites in the South West and, small though it is, may have been used for dehusking prepared grain prior to grinding or for crushing malted barley or perhaps for deshelling nuts. Charred cereal grains and seeds of weeds of cultivation as well as charred hazelnut shells were found within the ash in the gully. The shape of the gully is interesting. The southern end of the gully was bowl-like, its base apparently baked. It then narrowed for a length of about two metres before widening out again in the central part of the feature to a width of about 1.5 metres. Only the base of the bowl showed signs of high temperature, and it may be that the whole arrangement was designed to channel hot air to the central area. The bowl had been sealed off with three large, flat stones and the quern stone appeared to have been deliberately placed beside it. Large stones had been dumped into the gully as far as the central area. Putting these factors together, it becomes possible to imagine that the gully had a role in the preparation of grain either for baking or for brewing. Whether the circular structure is also connected with such purposes is impossible to say. Perhaps comparable sites elsewhere will throw some light on this.

Plate 5.2
The saddle quern.
(scale 10cm)

We were able to recover enough organic matter to gain some idea of the Middle Bronze Age environment of this part of West Exmoor and the inhabitants' use of its resources. The analysis of pollen grains, charcoal and charred seeds and other scraps of plant material has enabled us to envisage the Middle Bronze Age activity taking place within an open environment dominated by grasses with heath conditions not far away, ie. an acid grass and heather community much as is found on Exmoor today. Fern and pine were also present. The predominance among the identified wood species of oak followed by hazel suggests preferential gathering of these species for fires and conceivably for other purposes too. It may also indicate a predominance of oak and hazel in the environment. Alder also had a significant presence and may be thought to have been gathered from beside the Heddon Stream in the valley below the site. Additional small quantities of willow (probably goat willow), hawthorn, ash and birch were brought in for burning. Surprising, considering its abundance today and its suitability as a fuel, was the limited presence of ash which was identified in only one sample.

Pollen of dandelion, daisy, ribwort plantain and seeds of dock are indicative of disturbed and trodden ground around the site, and the presence of weeds of cultivation together with charred grain suggests cereal cultivation nearby. The presence of orache and fat hen may be related to manuring with animal dung. No chaff was clearly identified, but the charred state of the grain and its accompanying weed seeds must indicate that at least the last stages of processing for use were taking place on site. The principal grain, among that which was recovered (both from dated Bronze Age and Iron Age contexts), was hulled wheat followed by barley (type not identified) and possibly oats. The exploitation of wild food sources was evidenced by the presence of charred hazelnut shells.

Environmental information such as this begins to provide an insight into Bronze Age life. An interesting aspect of Bronze Age behaviour is highlighted by evidence of the manner in which the settlement was abandoned. As indicated above, on Bronze Age sites in Cornwall, most especially at Trethellen Farm, near Newquay (Nowakowski 1991 & 2000), but at other Cornish sites also, certain features have been interpreted as evidence of deliberate and organised abandonment. These included the removal of posts and the blocking of post-holes with stones, the burying of hearths, the cleaning down of house sites and the significant placement of domestic objects. At Holworthy Farm we have seen something similar. Post-holes of the post-ring had had the posts removed and in some cases the holes had been blocked with a single stone, while others had been filled with the burnt remains of what may have been the post. The placing of a saddle-quern and of a pottery vessel have already been mentioned. In addition one post-hole contained a small stone tool which must have arrived there after the removal of the post, while in a shallow scoop was an assemblage of pottery sherds, a broken hammer stone and a broken 'loom weight', all apparently deliberately placed there. The ash which filled the gully discussed above may have arrived there as a result of a cleaning process, since mixed in with it were flint flakes and completed scrapers as well as the egg cases of a human intestinal parasite. The gully had been finally closed off with large stones dumped onto the ash. Finally, the group of pottery

Plate 5.3
Charred grain from the bottom of a post-hole, radio-carbon dated to cal.390-180 BC.

sherds found in the base of the second ash-filled gully may have been deliberately placed there. All of this lends itself to interpretation as evidence of acts of closure comparable with the Cornish sites.

An abandonment around 1100 BC may signal a climatic deterioration to which a settlement at this altitude would have been sensitive. A single radiocarbon date of around 900 BC suggests continued use of the site, but there is nothing to indicate any further significant activity until the third/fourth century BC. To this period we can confidently attribute one major post-hole because concealed beneath a flat stone near its base was a deposit of charred grain (Plate 5.3) – about an eggcupful – which yielded a radiocarbon date of cal. 390-180 BC. Such a deposit is more likely to be associated with foundation than departure, but unfortunately there is at present no further evidence of what might have been happening at this Iron Age period. By the time the Iron Age people came to use the site, the original occupants would have been lost to memory, though the enclosure was very probably still visible in the landscape and some echo of its former life may have continued to resonate in the district.

The question of continuity is one that continually fascinates and vexes landscape archaeologists. Recently gathered environmental evidence from moorland sites (see Fyfe, this volume) indicates a discontinuity of land management between the prehistoric period and the early Middle Ages. Whether or not this cultural change corresponds to ethnic change is open to debate. However, if a genealogical link is debatable, there may yet be a psychological link between the peoples of the Bronze Age and the Iron Age and their medieval successors. It seems improbable that the Iron Age use of the site was continuous with the earlier Bronze Age occupation; it is more likely that the Iron Age inhabitants of the area made their own use of the embanked enclosure on the hillside above the head-waters of the Heddon Stream. It was ready made for a settlement or at least for seasonal occupation or perhaps even (dare we say it?) for some ritual purpose. If it impressed itself on the consciousness of Iron Age people, it seems equally to have lurked on the edge of medieval Parracombe minds, if the field names as recorded for the tithe survey of the 1840s reflect historic perceptions of the landscape. In the tithe apportionment the field in which the enclosure is situated is called, quite explicably, 'Greenwell', a spring with surrounding sedgy ground being present in the field. The neighbouring field is called 'Holy Pound', a name for which the steep, scrubby ground suggests no reason. If however, we remove the skinny, probably 18th century hedge-bank between the fields and regard the area as a single piece, then the name 'Holy Pound' very probably refers to the enclosure, which, before it became ploughed almost flat, must have remained clearly visible. The term 'pound' in the field name recalls Dartmoor sites such as Grimspound or Ermepound, both of them Bronze Age enclosed settlements, while 'holy' is very unusual in field names, but occurs in a number of place names referring sometimes to church land, but usually to some object (e.g. a well, a stone) of pagan veneration. Whatever the explanation, the field name 'Holy Pound' which is still in use in the 21st century would seem to represent a folk memory of the significance of this place in the landscape.

The excavations carried out by NDAS have begun to breathe life into the relics of prehistoric life in the Exmoor region. There is a need now to follow this up with the detailed examination of other settlement remains both around Parracombe and farther afield in Greater Exmoor. Most of what is 'known' about the prehistory of North Devon and Exmoor is of a general nature based on analogy with other parts of the South West, largely Cornwall where archaeologists have been busy and very effective. It is time to get specific and to develop our own regional excavation strategy, so that North Devon and Exmoor ceases to be an archaeological black hole in the West Country.

6

An Iron Age roundhouse at Middle Burrow Farm, East Worlington

South West Archaeology

Summary

Excavation and monitoring by South West Archaeology in 2008 on land at Middle Burrow Farm, East Worlington (For location see Fig. 6.1) uncovered part of an Iron Age settlement. A series of stake- and post-holes and/or small pits were uncovered that were dated by ceramic and carbon-14 evidence to c.400 BC-AD 50. Most of the

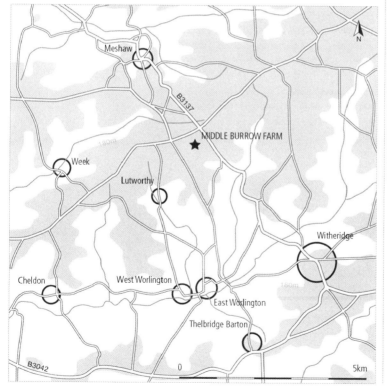

Fig.6.1:
Middle Burrow
Farm: Location map

features encountered lay within a penannular gully, 12.25m in diameter, interpreted as the foundation trench of an Iron Age roundhouse. In addition, two probable 'four-poster' structures were excavated, one of which clearly post-dated the roundhouse, indicating more than one phase of Iron Age activity on the site.

Introduction:

In March 2008 South West Archaeology was commissioned by the owners of Middle Burrow Farm, East Worlington, to carry out archaeological monitoring on the construction of a new dairy unit. This work was carried out at the request of Devon County Historic Environment Service. The mechanical stripping of topsoil from the site revealed numerous archaeological features which, upon excavation, proved to represent an Iron Age roundhouse and attendant structures, one of only a small number of examples in lowland Devon, and only the second Bronze Age/Iron Age roundhouse to be excavated in North Devon.

The site lies on the north side of the existing farm buildings (at NGR SS277207 117534). Prior to its development, the site was a permanent pasture that sloped down very gently to the south-west at an elevation of just under 220m AOD and with a total area of 2800m². The Devon Historic Landscape Characterisation Project characterises the area of the site as 'Medieval enclosures based on strip fields', and the site lies close to a scheduled ancient monument (no.30319), a 'round barrow cemetery on West Burrow Moor'. This scheduling covers six separate areas that protect the remains of seven Bronze Age bowl barrows. The closest of these lies only 100m north-north-east of the site, with the others spread out in an arc to the north and west.

The Excavation:

Mechanical stripping removed 0.3-0.4m of topsoil revealing a stony brownish-yellow undisturbed clay-silt subsoil, into which 45 archaeological features had been cut. Many of these were shallow – 0.1m deep or less – and most were under 0.3m (the deepest being 0.48m). This, and the absence of any archaeological surfaces on the undisturbed clay, suggests that the upper levels of the archaeology had been removed, ploughing being the most likely cause. All but one of the identified features were round or oval; the largest were 0.7m across, with most being considerably smaller. All are interpreted as post- or stake-holes or small pits. These features are described in four groups (below) relating to their position on the site (Fig. 6.2). Unless otherwise stated, all features were cut into the natural silt-clay and contained a single fill that was overlain by topsoil. Almost all the fills were greyish-brown clay-silts with stone inclusions.

All the pottery recovered was South Western Decorated (Glastonbury) Ware dating within the third to first centuries BC – the mid- to late Iron Age.

The Results:

On the eastern edge of the excavated area there were a number of cut features (Group 1: Fig. 6.3), some of which may have been part of a structure that extended beyond the edge of excavation. Prominent within this group was a setting of four post-holes with common characteristics (dimensions and presence of packing stones) suggesting

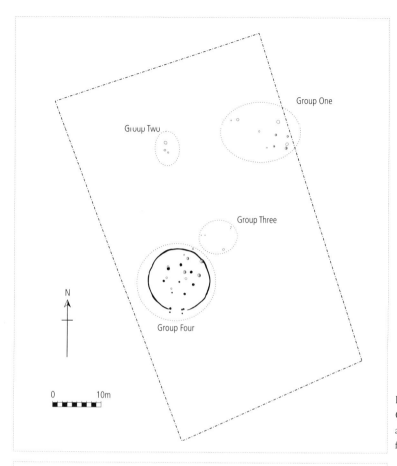

Group One

Group Two

Group Three

Group Four

N

0   10m

Fig.6.2:
General plan of
archaeological
features.

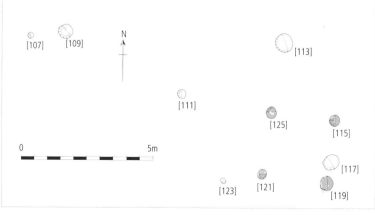

[107]   [109]

N

[113]

[111]

[125]

[115]

0   5m

[117]

[123]   [121]   [119]

Fig.6.3: Group 1
features: The
shading denotes the
'four-poster'.

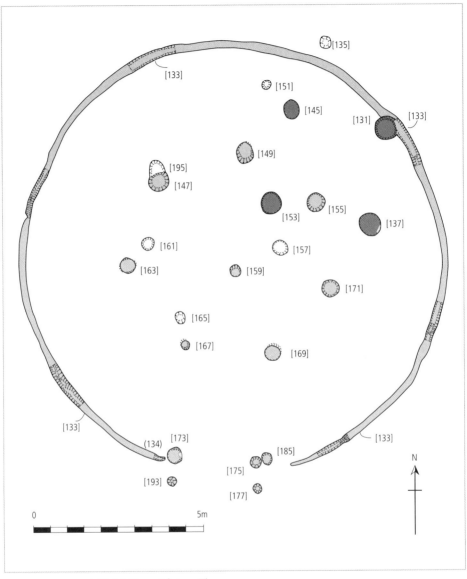

Fig.6.4: Group 4 features: The light grey shading denotes elements of the roundhouse and the dark grey the 'four-poster'. (Figures in square brackets denote cut features: see text)

that they represented the main supports of a small, square timber-framed building.

Other clusters of truncated post- and stake-holes (Groups 2 and 3) did not lend themselves to interpretation. On the western side of the excavated area, however, Group 4 (Fig. 6.4) conveyed a great deal of information. The major feature here was a steep-sided penannular gully [133] 12.25m in diameter. In the base of this feature were a number of shallow post-holes and sub-rectangular slots that are interpreted as the sockets for posts and planks, indicating that this gully formed the foundation trench for the outer wall of a roundhouse. In the south-west quadrant of the gully there was a gap 3.6m wide that was flanked by a setting of four post-holes, likely to be the remains of a porch. The north-eastern member of this group of four [175] had a flanking post-hole [185], which might have represented a replacement or reinforcement. The gully became narrower and shallower either side of the porch. Inside the gully was a ring 6m in diameter comprising of seven post-holes, with another post-hole roughly at the centre, indicating the roof of the roundhouse was supported by a ring of posts and possibly a central post.

Also within this group was a setting of four post-holes describing a small square building 3.30m by 3.30m, similar to the identified structure in Group 1. It was evident that this structure post-dated the roundhouse, since one of its post-holes [131] cut the edge of the penannular gully, thereby suggesting the period of occupation extended beyond the life of the roundhouse. Similarly there was at least one cut feature, a shallow pit [195], which was cut by one of the post-holes [147] of the inner ring of the roundhouse, implying activity that pre-dated the building. Thus there is evidence of an extended period of occupation.

Sherds of pottery were found within both [147] and [195]. The two sherds found within the fill of [147] included a rim. The fill of [131] contained 10 sherds of pottery including a decorated body-sherd and a rim. The fills of post-holes [137] and [145] contained one and two fragments respectively. The rims and decorated body-sherd lend themselves to dating on stylistic grounds (see below).

Conclusions

The features and the pottery excavated at Middle Burrow Farm, East Worlington indicate Iron Age occupation at the site. All but one of the features uncovered were discrete post-holes or small pits, but it is still possible to infer, from fortuitous inter-cutting, at least three phases:

1. The shallow pit [195] comes from a period of activity pre-dating the roundhouse as it is cut by [147], one of the inner ring of postholes.

2. The roundhouse itself is clearly visible from its outer foundation trench [133], inner ring of postholes and porch.

3. A square four-poster structure post-dates the roundhouse, its eastern post [131] cutting the penannular gully [133]. The four-poster structure that lay 26m to the north-east of the roundhouse had no stratigraphic relationships that would have allowed phasing.

The ceramic evidence suggests a mid- to late Iron Age date for the activity on this site (third to first centuries BC), but the pottery does not allow the individual phases to be more closely dated. Radiocarbon dates obtained from the site confirm it was occupied c.400-200 BC, but again, do not clarify the phasing. The C14 date for the penannular gully is earlier (311-209 cal BC at 64.8% reliability) than for the porch or the inner circle of post-holes (196-53 and 191-51 cal BC at 95.4% reliability), but the stratigraphically later four-poster produced a similar date (204-52 cal BC at 94.7% reliability). This would indicate there is an issue with residuality on site.

With an internal diameter of 12.25m the roundhouse is at the larger end of the scale for such structures although examples over 15m in diameter have been excavated. A roundhouse of similar size was reconstructed at Castell Henllys, Pembrokeshire (based on excavated evidence) although this had a free-spanning roof rather than an inner ring of postholes. Another reconstruction of a similar size based upon an example from Pimperne, Dorset, did have an inner ring of posts; however, the diameter of this was 9.75m compared to 6m at Middle Burrow Farm. It is evident that this example fits into the pattern of considerable variation on the basic roundhouse plan.

The outer wall of the roundhouse sat within a foundation trench. Recent studies of the evidence from numerous excavations show this is the case with the majority of roundhouses (as opposed to posts with wattle-and-daub panels or stone walling) and it is thought that the walls set in such trenches would be made of split timbers. As noted above, the base of the trench had both circular and sub-rectangular depressions within it. The former may be the points where the bases of posts rested whilst the latter are interpreted as slots for planks and these measured 0.15m to 0.20m by 0.05m. Two of these possible plank slots overlap each other clinker fashion but an adjacent slot does not; the impression is that the planks were arranged in a somewhat irregular manner, gaps probably being sealed with daub. As noted above, the penannular gully grew shallower and narrower either side of the gap for the porch, which may suggest the wall was less substantial at this point. The inner posts of the porch may have supported the roof at this point.

Studies of large numbers of roundhouses have shown that most porches face the quadrant between north-east and south-east, benefiting from optimum sunlight as well as shelter from prevailing westerly winds. While it is not unusual to encounter south-west facing doorways, it is not common. The orientation of the porch of the Middle Burrow roundhouse might have been favourable for allowing natural light into the structure during the middle of the day through to the afternoon, but would have been less sheltered from the prevailing winds than an east-facing opening would be. It would, however, have afforded clear views of Yes Tor and High Willhays, prominent high points of Dartmoor 20 miles away. This may be coincidental but there might also be aesthetic or religious/cultural motivation for choosing this view. Unfortunately the construction of modern farm buildings to the south has obscured the original vista.

If the corners of the porch are also the door posts (and there are no other suitable features) then this implies a doorway some 3m across, and this would be wider than average. However, the door posts may have been supported on a structure such as a sill beam, any signs of which would not have survived truncation. The presence of what may be a replacement or reinforcement for one of the corner posts of the porch fits with observations in experimental reconstructions of roundhouses that the porches are particularly prone to wind damage and often require repair.

The presence of a posthole near the centre of the building was noted above. Experimental reconstructions have shown that a central post is very useful to aid the positioning of the rafters during the construction of the roofs of large roundhouses; the post does not need to be maintained once the roof is complete. Because of the truncation across the site there are no remains at Middle Burrow of internal features such as a hearth or any sort of flooring.

The four-posters at Middle Burrow fall into a category of structures common on Iron Age sites. These are usually interpreted as raised granaries, small buildings 2m-4m across supported by four substantial posts, implying that they were built to carry a considerable load. This is certainly the case at Middle Burrow Farm: the four-poster within the roundhouse had post-pipes that were 0.47m and 0.44m in diameter. There were no clear post-pipes for the four-poster in the north-east of the site, although the presence of packing stones in the post-holes suggests timbers around 0.3m in diameter. An alternative explanation sometimes offered for four-posters is that of watchtowers, which seems less probable at East Worlington on an apparently undefended piece of sloping ground.

As noted (above) the Middle Burrow site is adjacent to a Bronze Age barrow cemetery. Four barrows lie in a rough east-to-west line about 150m to the north of the roundhouse and three more are sited 300-450m away to the west-south-west. All but one of these are still upstanding features, the largest being 1.40m high. It can be assumed that they were even more prominent in the Iron Age landscape and formed part of the everyday life and experience of the occupants of the roundhouse. We can only speculate upon what significance they may have placed upon these monuments and whether they related them to previous inhabitants of the area, possibly even regarding them as the burial place of direct ancestors. Likewise, it is impossible to know the reason for directing the roundhouse doorway toward the high points of Dartmoor although it seems likely that this was of some importance as such an orientation into the prevailing wind is generally rare.

Particularly on a site lacking a clear boundary or enclosure such as this, it is difficult to ascertain whether past activity extended beyond the excavated area. One of the four-posters and the roundhouse itself lie on the very edge of the excavated area and it is possible that more structures lie beneath farmland or the agricultural buildings nearby. Certainly the presence of a four-poster post-dating the roundhouse implies occupation beyond the abandonment of that house and the possibility of more dwellings in the vicinity.

In summary, the excavations at Middle Burrow, East Worlington revealed at least part of a mid- to late Iron Age settlement that seems to have persisted long enough for a roundhouse to be abandoned and another structure built on its site. The excavation of any settlement of this period away from the high ground of Exmoor and Dartmoor is rare in the county of Devon.

7

Ancient Hoofprints at Northam Burrows

Based on A.J. Passmore, Exeter Archaeology 2009

In March 2008 severe storms and high tides damaged the pebble ridge on the foreshore at Northam Burrows and caused the dunes to retreat, in places by up to 25m. The scouring of the pebble ridge exposed deposits of clay, sand and silts, preserved in part of which were hoof prints (Plate 7.1). These were observed by local resident Sarah Gallifent who took photographs and reported the find to the Museum of Barnstaple and North Devon. Subsequently Exeter Archaeology were commissioned by Devon County Council to record and investigate the exposed deposits and to obtain reports on any environmental materials – charcoal flecks, pollen, diatoms and foraminifera (water-borne micro-organisms) - that might be preserved. The fact that the exposed deposits lay some 2.5km north-east of the submerged Mesolithic deposits at Westward Ho! initially seemed to offer the possibilty of learning more about the environment of the Mesolithic site.

Unfortunately between the time of first reporting and the time the survey commenced, tidal action had already eroded part of the layer in which the hoofprints were preserved. Fortunately Sarah Gallifent's photographs show them as first exposed. They are evidently the hoofprints of cloven-hooved ungulates, very probably deer, but it has not been possible to determine the species. A small area of the prints was lifted for possible display at a later date in the Museum of Barnstaple and North Devon. There were no artifacts present and the environmental samples did not yield

Plate 7.1
Ancient hoofprints probably of deer revealed after storm damage to the pebble ridge at Northam Burrows. (Photo: Sarah Gallifent)

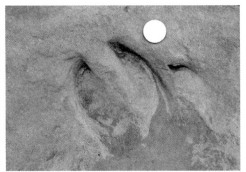

Plate 7.2
Tim Gent of Exeter
Archaeology
working out how to
preserve the
hoofprints.
(Photo: Exeter
Archaeology)

any material which might be suitable for carbon dating. It is clear that the hoofprints were made before the pebble ridge and dunes formed at this location, but the fact that the layer in which they were made lies 4m higher than the deposits at Westward Ho! and is of a different character makes it probable that the animals were here at a much later, possibly medieval, date.

Nevertheless the evidence of the environmental samples sketches a picture of a different environment from that of the present. Four layers were identified the lowest of which (Layer 4), containing the hoofprints, was a grey, sandy clay above which were deposits of yellow sand alternating with silts. The uppermost layer (Layer 1) was a grey, sandy silt with some charcoal flecks. Floated samples of the charcoal were sent for analysis, but the material was too slight to yield any information. From the same layer (Layer 1) pollen samples were also taken for the examination of preserved pollen and spores. Although the pollen was sparse, it was possible to identify tree, herb and fern species. These suggested that at the time Layer 1 developed this was most probably a salt-marsh environment in which grew Chenopodiaceae (goosefoots, oraches and glassworts), Lactucoideae (dandelion type) and Poaceae (grasses) as well as salt tolerant plants such as thrift or sea lavender and sea plantain. Ferns, bracken and sphagnum moss were also present. At a distance was woodland with elm, oak, alder and hazel. Diatoms proved to be absent, but the foraminifera present indicated an intertidal, probably salt-marsh, situation. All or most of the environmental information came from Layer 1, the highest layer. The sandy clay in which the hoofprints were left was unfortunately devoid of any pollen, so that we are denied information on the development of the salt-marsh environment.

Disappointing as it is to have no information relating directly to the environment at the time when the animals were here, it is nevertheless possible to say that at that period the area was subject to episodes of flooding with the deposition of water-borne silts alternating with the accumulation of wind-blown sand. The hoofprints were consequently sealed beneath mixed silt and sand deposits on which a salt-marsh plant community developed, presumably when the sea-level had not yet reached its present post-glacial extent.

(For the full account see Exeter Archaeology Report No. 09/70: A.J.Passmore)

8

Mines, Mills and Monasteries: A volunteer's account of digging at Combe Martin

Mary (Flowa) Houldsworth

Today, Combe Martin is a popular holiday resort, famous for its carnival and the Earl of Rone celebration. However, beneath its darkest depths, a kaleidoscope of history is beginning to reveal a very varied industrial and commercial past in which mining for silver has alternated with growing hemp for sailcloth, and rope and, more recently, growing strawberries.

For over eight years, Trevor Dunkerley, an archaeologist who lives in the village, has been researching the history of mining and also, among other things, the possible existence of a fulling-mill -or tucking-mill as they are more usually known in Devon. The Domesday Book makes no mention of any mill in Combe Martin, however later records mention tucking-mills and grist-mills as well as a water-driven grindstone and malt-mills located somewhere in the village. Fulling is one of the processes through which woollen cloth goes before it is ready for use. The earliest fulling process involved scouring and cleansing the raw cloth by trampling on it in a tub of water and urine and fullers earth, a fine clay. Later the 'trampling' was done by wooden hammers in a water-driven fulling-mill. After fulling the cloth was hung to dry on tenterhooks, suspended on a wooden frame or rack.

A party of volunteers joined Trevor in his investigations and the search for a fulling-mill took a new turn when Margaret Reed, a local historian, provided assistance, and discovered documentary evidence of a number of fulling- or tucking- and grist-mills in Combe Martin. A lengthy deed of 1702 mentioned, among 43 separate properties in Combe Martin, a hemp pool *near the tucking mill leat by the way leading towards Eastacott in the possession of John Thorne* (NDRO B9/5/31). The same document mentioned hemphays, hemp gardens and hemplands at numerous locations in the parish. As the production of hemp fibre was an important industry in Combe Martin and as the production of hemp fibre involved soaking for lengthy periods in water the search for a hemp-pool was added to the search for a fulling mill.

The leat mentioned in the document could be traced. It ran from the top of Chapel Lane, along Watery Lane, through a deep cutting made through the Devonian shillet at Corner Lane and across the fields to Mine Tenement, the water supply being constant and plentiful throughout the year. As the North Devon Journal in 1845 had reported the drowning of the mine blacksmith's four year old son in the mill pond, the evidence began to point towards Mine Tenement.

Mine Tenement is among the sites on the northern valley slopes of Combe Martin where there is evidence of intermittent silver/lead mining. The earliest record of silver/lead mining in Combe Martin dates from 1292. The Black Death brought a stop to it in the 14th century, and then it continued intermittently in a 'boom and bust' fashion up to the 19th century (Claughton 2003). It is thought that during the poor years, the growing of hemp and the production of rope, sails and cobblers thread offered employment for the villagers.

Hemp, or *cannabis sativa*, has been cultivated in England since at least AD 800 (Godwin 1967, 42-8 and 137-8), mainly for its fibre, which was used to make sails, ropes, fishing nets and clothes. Combe Martin being a coastal settlement which was always difficult of access by land, hemp production must have been important. Hemp cultivation may have reached its peak during the early 16th century when Henry VIII decreed that increased hemp production was required to supply the expanding navy.

Turning the hemp stalks into fibre and thread involves what is known as 'retting', a process which softens the fibres into malleable strands for the production stages. Bundles of hemp stems are bound together in a similar way to sheaves of corn, and laid in alternate rows along the base of a hemp pool. After soaking, the valuable hemp fibres can be separated from the stalks, while the water, which now contains toxins, has to be released safely to prevent any contamination of drinking water sources.

Both fulling and retting require water and imply a pool or pond and the documents, together with knowledge of the course of the leat, seemed to suggest that Mine Tenement was the place to look. The matter was discussed with the Combe Martin Silver Mines Research Group who own Mine Tenement and in 2003 it was agreed that exploration should begin.

Plate 8.1: View of the 'hemp pool' from the west showing the buttresses and the drain outflow.

Survey and Excavation:

During 2003 to 2005 geophysical surveys were carried out across the entire field. Trevor Dunkerley, inspired and directed the excavations, initiating the digging of a 2m x 2m test pit, which revealed only mining spoil. On a walk over the site in 2005 with Anne Todd from Tiverton Archaeology Group, it suddenly became apparent that lying beneath a grassy track lay a large stone, which was quite unexpected in a field

43

that had formerly been a vegetable garden. The trowels probed, and to our great surprise, revealed the remains of a robbed-out wall, something which had not shown up on the geophysical surveys. Serious excavation now commenced.

When exposed the 0.5m wide wall footing was found to run east-west, and then to take a 115° turn to the south (Plate 8.1). Subsequently a second solid wall was excavated, running parallel to and 0.2m apart from the first wall and likewise turning through 115°, and extending down to bedrock. Abutting this wall were sediments, apparently from a pond, in which eighteen separate deposits could be distinguished. The wall apparently was the boundary of a pond, but a mystery emerged with the excavation of three *internal* buttresses measuring approximately 1 meter in thickness, two abutting the north wall and (as far as we know so far), one situated on the east wall.

This mysterious arrangement became even more interesting when, visiting the site in May, 2007, Dr (now Professor) Steve Rippon of Exeter University suggested that the structure was so solidly built that it might be monastic in origin. The possibility of monastic influence induced us to spread our research net yet further afield, in fact to Lewes in Sussex. Since a connection between Combe Martin and the Cluniac priory of St Mary Magdalene in Barnstaple had already come to light in a separate piece of research, it was suggested that the priory might well have a daughter or satellite cell situated near a wealthy silver/lead source in the area. The Cartulary of the

Cluniac Priory at Lewes (the mother house in England) proved incredibly helpful, citing a dispute in 1133 between the Monks of the Chapel of Combe Martin and Berrynarbor over a parcel of land. According to the record the Prior of Lewes had disputed with Robert, son of Martin (of Combe Martin) over the ownership of a ferling of land within the manor, the Prior claiming that it belonged to the order's church in Berrynarbor. The monks lost, but Robert then generously granted them half a ferling of land in his manor. This was proof that the Cluniac order held land in Combe Martin, so could well have supervised the construction of the present structures.

External buttresses are common on religious buildings; however, internal buttresses are rare, and these were inexplicable on this site, unless we return to the production of hemp and the processes involved. Based on the dimensions of the excavated structure, the volume of water contained would have been at least 187 cubic metres (ie. 187 metric tonnes!) which all had to be drained off periodically. Maybe the internal buttresses acted as structural protection to prevent the walls collapsing during the frequent water-draining process?

Thursday October 12th 2007, dawned cool and fresh, as diggers began the day's excavations, when volunteer Michelle Thomas suddenly exclaimed that her trowel had tapped a metal object! Tools down, we watched her slowly uncover a cast-iron circular band which encased the remains of an elm lined drainage channel. The pool outlet system lay just 0.7m below the initial surface of the dig! A second identical cast iron ring, with a diameter of 0.3m supported on a wooden base and spaced 0.36m from the first, led to a drainage channel 1.4m in length. Interestingly, the channel exited through both stone walls, indicating that they were contemporary. Clive Comer continued excavating the channel (Plate 8.2) and found it lined with non-local stone and gradually narrowing. Clive was able to chase it as far as the field boundary, but its final destination is unknown. Dendrochronology (tree-ring dating) has since established a felling date of AD1240 for the elm.

To date, three corners have been excavated, showing a parallelogram-shaped pool. However, although the origin and the course of the leat have been traced, the leat inlet remains elusive.

At present excavation and research continue to unearth the history and archaeology of this fascinating site. It is thought that during the 13th – 15th centuries the pond may have provided a water source for a fulling mill, when the woollen industry moved from towns to water sources in the countryside. Whatever its original purpose, it may well have taken on differing roles throughout its existence, alternating between hemp retting pool, fulling mill pond and finally, during the 19th century, a source of water power for the mining industry when Woolmers Gazette recoded in 1816 the sale of *a nearly new iron water wheel for sale along with all machinery and 100 fathoms of flat rods.* It is believed that this 20 foot iron wheel replaced the existing fulling-mill wheel to drive the 50 fathoms of flat iron rods pumping water from Director's Shaft.

Hand digging of the huge amount of overburden has unearthed not only the waste products of lead smelting and silver refining and debris from the blacksmith's workshop, but also an interesting array of artefacts. These include part of a brass navigational hinged divider and three inscribed brass buttons bearing three different inscriptions which, it has been suggested, identify them as manufactured by the Hudson Bay Company between 1830-35, and possibly adorned a rifleman's tunic during the American Civil War (what are they doing here??).

Among the special pottery finds are two Bronze Age pot sherds (identified by Henrietta Quinell of Exeter University) from the topsoil, a 9th century Saxon sherd discovered in the lowest silt of the pool, a 12th century handmade pot strap handle with markings, 12th and 13th century rhenish ware, 13th - 15th century sherds from an Exmoor source and fragments of a 16th-17th century Iberian olive jar from the area of Cadiz.

Most interesting for the miners were two pieces of the rare 'Fahlerz Ore'. Fahlerz is a German word meaning: 'dull ore'. It is very fine grained and dull in colour compared with the more frequently found coarse grained bright ore. It is the richest ore containing 16% silver, with inclusions of tetrahydrite of copper, which is only visible under a microscope. It was identified by Bastian Asmus at the UCL Institute of Archaeology.

The last known working of the silver/lead mines was in 1888, after which the mine spoil and blacksmiths wastes were tipped into the redundant pond and covered with top soil and returned to agriculture. The filled pond ended its days as a fruit and vegetable garden - until local archaeologists and volunteers arrived, towels in hand, to unearth the secrets of its fascinating former lives.

The excavation is a Community Archaeology Initiative and is inclusive and accessible to any person who has an interest in archaeology.

9

The Past, Present and Future of Palaeoenvironmental Research in North Devon

Ralph Fyfe and Heather Adams
School of Geography, University of Plymouth, Plymouth

Palaeoenvironmental research in North Devon is dominated by the study of the upland of Exmoor and its hinterland. Modern administrative boundaries have resulted in the division of the upland between North Devon and West Somerset; for the purposes of this paper both areas will be included as it makes little sense to discuss only one part of a larger whole. Reference will also be made to recent work in Mid-Devon, around Rackenford. This is one of the few 'lowland' areas in which palaeoenvironmental studies have actually been undertaken and published in the region, and as such is invaluable in realising what the world beyond the upland was like.

The polarisation of research on the upland perhaps requires some explanation. Why has there been little research in the lowland, in spite of advances in understanding over the last 20 years through archaeological survey in these areas (in particular recognition of important prehistoric complexes though cropmarks)? The answer lies in the existence and preservation of sites which preserve palaeoecological sequences. Without these sites there is little or no potential for palaeoenvironmental research. On-site archaeological contexts with palaeoenvironmental potential are likely to be found across the region, but little developer-funded excavation or archaeological research projects means that these contexts are still waiting to be discovered. The uplands, however, contain a glut of possible sites within the peat-covered landscapes, at a variety of scales, from small wetlands to large expansive blanket bog. As a consequence, off-site palaeoenvironmental research has in effect defaulted to the uplands.

The earliest research in the region was undertaken on the blanket peat of Exmoor as part of doctoral research by Merryfield (1977), although only one main sequence was radiocarbon dated, at the Chains (Merryfield and Moore, 1974). After a lull, there followed the examination of peat in the intertidal zone at Westward Ho!, which remains one of the only integrated archaeological and palaeoenvironmental excavations in North Devon (Balaam et al., 1987). Further work on Exmoor followed in the late 1980s, at Hoar Moor (Francis and Slater, 1990) and Codsend Moor (Francis and Slater, 1992). The most intensive phase of research began in the late 1990s, and has continued through to the present day. This began with further doctoral work (Fyfe, 2000) on a river catchment scale (Fyfe et al., 2003a), and led to a programme of palaeoenvironmental work across Mid- to North Devon (as part of a Greater Exmoor project) which focussed on the development of medieval farming systems in the South West (Fyfe et al., 2003b; Fyfe et al., 2004; Rippon et al., 2006). Almost all of this work has been the study of pollen from the sediments, recording vegetation changes as a proxy for human manipulation and management of the landscape.

It is not the purpose of this paper to review in detail the results of these projects, and in part this is being presented elsewhere (Fyfe, in review). Rather, some key observations can be made about the current state of knowledge of the past environment of North Devon. First, our understanding of the development of the lowlands is poor, particularly for prehistory. The research in Mid-Devon around Rackenford and Knowstone Moors (Fyfe et al., 2004) is limited to an understanding of the last 2500 years. Lowland work further south, in the Exe valley above Exeter, is from wide gravel terraces. These are likely to be unrepresentative of the majority of lowland Devon. Second, there is still much to be learnt on the uplands, in spite of the overwhelming focus on this landscape. Few Mesolithic sequences, comparable to the coastal sections, have been identified and studied. Of more importance, perhaps, is that the relationships between the changes that are evident from pollen-based studies and from the standing archaeology are tentative. This is as much the fault of the archaeology as the palaeoecology, with little or no chronological control on some of the key monument types that are common on the upland (Riley and Wilson-North, 2001), and often the chronologies that do exist are based on comparisons from outside the immediate region.

Current research projects and challenges

As outlined in the previous section, the bread and butter of palaeoenvironment research within North Devon has been the study of landscape change through pollen analysis. To a greater or lesser extent this continues to be the case, although the rationale behind current projects moves beyond simply developing long palaeoenvironmental sequences. Indeed, with the exception of early prehistory, it could be argued that we already have a reasonable understanding of the broad-brush periods of landscape change. Instead, we should focus on key questions and key transitions in the archaeology and environment of the region. There are at present three main projects on-going ('live' in 2008/9) which have at least some palaeoenvironmental input and attempt to do just this. Two of these are integrated archaeological and palaeoenvironmental projects (Exmoor Miniliths Project and Exmoor Iron [ExFe]), the third has a strong conservation focus (Sustainable Management of Upland Peat Project).

The two integrated projects are examples of what might be achieved with concerted efforts to undertake interdisciplinary studies. The Exmoor miniliths project, directed by Mark Gillings (University of Leicester), is still in its infancy, but aims to understand the enigmatic stone settings and rows on Exmoor. Key to the success of the project will be the ability to develop strong chronologies for monuments and embed them in their contemporary landscape context through local palaeoenvironmental sequences of comparable age. This will present a raft of challenges, not least of which will be dating the stone settings; however, without an integrated approach, extracting meaning from either data set (the archaeology or the palaeoenvironment) remains impossible. The Exmoor Iron project, directed by Gill Juleff (University of Exeter) is at a more advanced stage, and the role of palaeoenvironmental studies is primarily to supplement the excavation chronologies and to assess the level of sustainability of production. The application of geochemical stratigraphies in peat bogs is a corner stone of this work, using the assumption that atmospheric pollutants produced as a by-product of smelting and iron processing (e.g. lead and copper) can be identified within the peat: peaks and troughs in the abundance of these metals can relate directly to intensity of metal working activities in the local landscape.

The third strand of current efforts on Exmoor at present surrounds how best to protect and value the environmental archaeological potential of our peatlands, a topic that resonates beyond the immediate region. Well-intentioned bog restoration projects which may disturb the peat matrix may not always fully realise the multiple values of peat on uplands for archaeology: (i) as a protective blanket which seals and preserves prehistoric and historic land surfaces; (ii) as a landscape within which past human activities took place, the remains of which may be preserved; (iii) as a medium within which the important palaeoecological resources are preserved; and (iv) as a record of past exploitation of the peat as a resource in itself, through the earthworks of peat ties and ditches. It is, of course, difficult to prove the potential of the first two of these categories, and this remains one of the great challenges for the landscape archaeologist. However, cairn fields have been demonstrated underneath blanket peat in the north west of England (Jamie Quatermaine, pers. comm.), an extensive Neolithic fieldsystem under peat is known from western Ireland (Ceida Fields, Co. Mayo: Caulfield, 1978), and closer to home, stone monuments have been revealed in (not beneath or on) blanket peat on Dartmoor, so why not on Exmoor? Novel techniques for survey, such as ground penetrating radar, may offer some of the best opportunities for exploring this avenue of archaeology further.

Palaeoecological sites have now been recognised as an integral part of the archaeology of the region, and as a consequence there is a need to be able to manage and preserve them effectively (Fyfe, 2006). The Sustainable Management of Upland Peat project is assessing the general condition of the palaeoenvironmental resource on Exmoor, with a view to making management recommendations for best practice preservation of the more valuable peatland archives. The project will develop a database of all high potential palaeoecological sequences on Exmoor (through extensive fieldwork), and establish the condition of this widespread resource through both extensive and intensive work. Visible damage to the upper sections of peat is assessed in the field, and a multi-strand approach to the preservation of the palaeoecological resource (i.e. the pollen grains and similar sub-fossils) is being undertaken. Long-term monitoring of water table fluctuations is being carried out to assess whether or not conditions are favourable for the preservation of the organic remains, alongside assessment of the actual condition of the remains themselves. A more sophisticated, evidence-based understanding of the threats to and condition of our upland peat will enable effective management for the longer term conservation of the resource.

Future directions

The greatest challenge for palaeoenvironmental research within North Devon at present is integrating the archaeological record with the palaeoecological record. This means that we should attempt to understand the archaeology better, with focussed excavations to attempt to establish chronologies for monuments. Detailed palaeoecological analysis targeted at key archaeological horizons and periods can then resolve the impacts of human societies on their landscape. The uplands probably offer the best opportunities for this type of work, and although this may perpetuate the upland/lowland divide in archaeological knowledge, it is perhaps debatable to what extent this division was recognisable, certainly within prehistory. The extent of relict field systems on Exmoor, both prehistoric (albeit surviving in fragmentary form today) and medieval, suggests that all of Exmoor was part of a productive agricultural system in the past. The spread of prehistoric 'ritual' monuments does not indicate any areas of the upland that were explicitly avoided: the blanks are as likely to reflect the distribution of later peat growth as the original distribution of sites. We should aim to encourage effective collaborative programmes of excavation and palaeoecological sampling.

It will not be easy to realise this ambition, and it is reliant on the discovery or recognition of key sites that allow an integrated approach, offering both chronological and palaeoecological potential. The application of innovative survey techniques (such as ground penetrating radar) may be a fruitful approach in peatland environments where sites may be preserved within or under peat. Such sites have tremendous potential (if they can be found!) for enhancing the understanding of the archaeology of the region. This effort should not detract from a need for better baseline knowledge of those archaeological periods poorly represented in the palaeoecological record, and in particular the Mesolithic and early Neolithic. These will have been key periods of time for the transformation of the whole landscape, from the so-called wildwood, or pre-landnam vegetation, to the open landscapes seen by the start of the Bronze Age. These are periods for which the archaeology is likely to be most elusive (although the excellent sites at Westward Ho! and Hawkcombe Head add much to our understanding of the later Mesolithic) and palaeoecology has most to offer in terms of landscape transformation.

10
Badges of Self-Esteem; An Assessment of Bottle Seals from North Devon

Chris Preece

INTRODUCTION

Bottle seals are the marks (usually initials, names, symbols or coats of arms) impressed by moulds onto the neck or body of bottles. Many carry dates and are therefore potentially useful for dating 17th to 19th century contexts. Undated examples can also be given date ranges based on bottle typology, or style of lettering on seals. Whilst a number have been recorded in archaeological contexts, many have been found by members of the public and donated to museums. Some end up in private collections and can be more difficult to access. Intact sealed bottles, in particular, are highly prized by collectors. Details of these can sometimes be gleaned from the catalogues of major auction houses. Members of the collecting fraternity have however, published much valuable research (e.g. Dumbrell 1983).

The earliest extant seals date from the mid-17th century and continue generally until the advent of moulded bottles in the 1820s, with one sealed example from North Devon as late as 1837.

Ruggles-Brise, in her seminal publication 'Sealed Bottles', 'had an idea that there were more of these (sealed bottles) in the western counties than elsewhere' (1949, 22). Dumbrell (op. cit) updated her list and it does show a high proportion from the West Country, in particular Devon.

Background

The finding of two bottle seals on separate watching briefs carried out by South West Archaeology in North Devon prompted further research. The area museums provided a number of additional examples, the majority of which were personal as opposed to 'tavern' seals. The only stratified seal was that of 'Nathaniel Cox 1716' from the Potters Lane site, Barnstaple (Blanchard, 1990). Quite a number of others have been found in topsoil. This might suggest curation as keepsakes or playthings, following bottle breakage. Their appeal today is a reflection of the fact that rarely can an archaeological artefact be attributed with certainty to a particular individual. This is often the case with bottle seals and documentary evidence can further flesh out the facts.

Nobility, Gentry, Clergy ... and the Middling Sort

In our era of 'lifestyle marketing' and 'social mobility', it is interesting to speculate on whether the archaeological record can be used to detect similar trends. Whilst there are examples of 'branding' (i.e. manufacturers' seals) amongst bottle producers in the 18th and 19th centuries, the marketing strategies of the businesses are difficult to discern. The motives of their customers however, are sometimes documented, or can at least be gleaned from the additional evidence of personal seals. A primary motive for all must have been self-esteem, even for the aristocracy for whom social esteem was already established. Their standing in the upper echelon would have been enhanced by the undoubted quality of seals executed by skilled (and probably more expensive) engravers. Two fine examples from North Devon were found during watching briefs carried out by South West Archaeology.

The first was located during the excavation of service trenches for new drains in the late 18th century stable block at Youlston Park, Shirwell in 2005. The trenches mainly followed the lines of the former stone flagged gutters which were blocked with silty clay in which the seal (Plate 10.1) was found (S.W.Arch. 2006). Its coat of arms is similar to a depiction inside the house at Youlston and conforms to Fox-Davies' description of the Chichester heraldry as 'chequy or and gules' (a chequered pattern, gold and red) with a crest as 'a heron rising with an eel in its beak proper' (1929, 361). Drake's genealogy lists a number of baronets (1886, 252-3). If the seal is contemporary with the stable block then there are two feasible owners of it: Sir John Chichester, 5th bart. (d. 1784) and Sir John Chichester, 6th bart (d. 1808).

Plate 10.1
Chichester seal from
Youlston

Plate 10.2
Luttrell seal from
Berry House

Plate 10.3
Chichester/Rolle
seal (Barnstaple
Museum)

Plate 10.4
'I. Kingdon 1786'
(Torrington
Museum)

Plate 10.1

Plate 10.2

Plate 10.3

Plate 10.4

The second seal was found in topsoil stripping at Berry House (latterly a farm), Hartland in 2006 (Plate 10.2). During breaching of an adjacent hedgebank, late-18th century bottle fragments were found. These had been deliberately placed at the base of the structure, presumably to deter burrowing. This is only tenuous dating evidence for the seal however, which was found some thirty metres away in topsoil. The seal itself depicts the shield of the Luttrells, one of the principal Hartland families. It is described as 'or a bend between six martlets (birds) sable, a crescent for difference' (Tuckett c.1860, 49). The Luttrells' full coat of arms can be seen in Hartland Church and is illustrated in Hobbs (2005, 36) who also points out their association with Hartland Abbey. The abbey is less than a mile from Berry House and it is thought that the house was part of its original endowment. Nicholas Wolferstan took possession of Berry in the mid-18th century, encouraged, according to Chope, by his mother's sister, Mary Luttrell (1940, 144-5). He is thought to have extended and upgraded the house and it has been suggested that he brought finance for both the house and the abbey which underwent major alterations at this time (S.W.Arch. 2005). It is tempting to see the seal as representing the gift of an appreciative aunt.

A particularly well executed seal from the Museum of Barnstaple and North Devon (Plate 10.3) shows the chequered pattern of the Chichesters on the left (as the seal is viewed) and the arms of the Rolles on the right. The latter are described by Colby as 'Or, on a fesse dancett e (toothed band) between three billets azure (blue rectangles), each charged with a lion rampant of the first, as many bezants (gold coins), quartering' (1872, 244). The seal therefore can be interpreted as commemorating a

Plate 10.5

Plate 10.6

Plate 10.5
'Thos Stevens Esq 1819' (Torrington Museum)

Plate 10.6
'C Sweet' (South Molton Museum)

Plate 10.7

Plate 10.8

Plate 10.7
'Revd. T Melhuish Ashwater 1824' (Holsworthy Museum)

Plate 10.8
Dutch/Belgian seal from Higher Holworthy

marriage between a male member of the Chichesters and a female from the Rolles (Oliver 2002, 96). Both Drake and Vivian detail the union in 1664 of Sir John Chichester and Susannah, widow of Alexander Rolle of Parkgate in the parish of Tawstock (1886, 269; 1895, 653). The seal is thought to have come from Tawstock.

Another influential North Devon family represented on seals are the Bourchier Wreys. There are two identical seals in the Museum of Barnstaple and North Devon reading 'Sr BW 1786'. These are also thought to have come from Tawstock and must have belonged to Sir Bourchier Wrey, 7th bart. Coulter lists the succession of the family and notes the death of the sixth baronet in 1784 (1996, App. 5). The seventh baronet's commissioning of sealed bottles to celebrate his position was probably tempered by a disastrous fire a year later, in 1787, which almost totally destroyed the Elizabethan mansion. He built the present house shortly after (Coulter 1996, 45).

The commissioning of sealed bottles reflected a need which must have been common to all but the aristocracy – the acquisition of social esteem. This has always been one of the prime motives for buying luxury items and as Morgan notes, status symbols are not new to the twentieth century (1977, 7).

However, social esteem depends to a degree on exclusivity for effect. As personalised number plates proliferate, they also become less esteemed. The increase in popularity of sealed bottles may have had such repercussions. Although the dating of coats of arms on seals alone is still problematic, there is a suggestion, albeit based on a small sample, of two periods when they were in vogue in Devon: the end of the 17th century and the latter part of the 18th/ beginning of the 19th century.

If the proliferation of others' seals in the first half of the 18th century may have temporarily affected the aristocracy's penchant for the trend, it was undoubtedly good for the economy. Langford notes that in the 18th century, it was "the constant fidelity of the middling sort to the fashions and habits of their social superiors which sustained the commercial viability of leisure and luxury" (1988, 443).

Whilst a number of seals in North Devon may be aspirational, they also reflect the pride felt by people who succeeded in their field. One example is the seal of 'John Abbott' on a rare bottle known as a decanter onion. This can be seen in the Museum of Barnstaple and North Devon. The likely owner of the bottle was John Abbott the younger (1639 -1727), a renowned plasterer famed for his ornate ceilings. The commissioning of the sealed decanter reflects the self-esteem he felt towards the end of his career.

Personal seals of successful females are a rarity and an example in Great Torrington Museum is of particular interest. 'Eliz Reynolds' probably refers to the sister of Sir Joshua Reynolds, Elizabeth Reynolds, who lived in the town. She was abandoned by her husband (a former mayor and failed businessman) in 1775 and left to bring up seven children 'in a desperate state of poverty' (Alexander and Hooper 1948, 186). She is thought to have gone into business (Sue Scrutton pers. comm.) and evidently did well, as she not only supported her offspring but also her errant husband (who eventually returned home to be nursed by her until his death). Her seal reflects triumph over adversity and a degree of understandable self-congratulation.

Two identical examples from Torrington, 'I Kingdon 1786' (Plate 10.4), suggest an interesting candidate for ownership. A certain J. Kingdon was fined for selling leather not sealed in 1753 (Alexander and Hooper 1948, 176); in 1778 John Kingdon and others were fined for keeping bull dogs unmuzzled (ibid, 141). Perhaps the seal was an attempt to regain respectability.

Another seal from Torrington hints at more established social esteem (Plate 10.5). The use of Esq. by Thos Stevens on his seal of 1819 was to assume 'a category not lightly bestowed' (Wills 1974, 44). This may be the same Thomas Stevens who was recorder of Exeter and died in 1832 (Alexander and Hooper 1948, 224).

The Clergy

It might seem incongruous (in a profession normally defined by its humble and unworldly philosophy), for there to have been a number of members of the clergy who were partial to the self-advertisement of sealed bottles. One seal, 'I Richards 1717,' was probably commissioned by John Richards to commemorate his inauguration as rector of Kentisbury in that year. The commissioning of sealed bottles to celebrate an event has been documented by Dumbrell (1983, 309) who equates the date of 1727 on a Jonathan Swift sealed bottle with the date of the second edition of 'Gulliver's Travels'. Ruggles-Brise, who first floated the theory, gives a number of examples, from a marriage to a maiden speech in parliament (1949, 31).

A second seal, 'C Sweet' (Plate 10.6), also found at Kentisbury Rectory, belonged to the subsequent incumbent Charles Sweet, who was in post from 1776 to 1833.

Whilst some clergymen's seals were fairly modest in the 18th century, there seems to have been a tendency in the next century for greater self-advertisement. As Hoskins points out, parsons in this century were often well connected and had private means (1954, 300). They could also be well-rounded characters, such as R.S. Hawker the vicar of Morwenstow, who was also a poet and antiquary. On his seal his name is prefixed by 'Rev' (Dumbrell 1983, 271). Another unashamed example is from Holsworthy museum and belonged to the Revd. Thomas Melhuish (the younger) of Ashwater. It is dated 1824 (Plate 10.7). He was instituted in 1811 and succeeded his father of the same name (Melhuish 1991, 38). His name is listed in a record of rural deans who visited the parish of Black Torrington (Leeson Day 1934, 74).

CONCLUSIONS

Social networks

Given that sealed bottles were intended to impress, then it must have been primarily through social gatherings that the impression was made and aspiration engendered. Ruggles-Brise mentions an occasion at Mr. Poveys in Lincoln Fields, London where there were 'divers great lords to see his well-contriv'd cellar and the ranging of his wine bottles' (1949, 15). Other social networks would have provided opportunities for dissemination of the trend: the Barnstaple Turnpike Trust of 1827 lists two Bourchier Wreys, Thomas Stevens and Charles Sweet (Rogers 1942, 162-7); Pigot's trade directory, under the heading of 'Nobility, Gentry and Clergy', lists members of the Chichester, Bourchier Wrey and Sweet families (1830, 180).

Local regiments comprised a wider mix: farmers, merchants, tradesmen, bankers and ship-owners amongst others, demonstrating that 'In North Devon the farming community was at all levels closely interwoven with the world of trade' (Rowe 1994, 8). A seal in Barnstaple museum ('W Prole'), belonged to William Prole, yeoman, who was listed as a lieutenant in the Georgeham Volunteers in 1799.

Members of the clergy would obviously have interacted and as with Richards and Sweet of Kentisbury, the fashion for sealed bottles might be passed on.

Trade

The importance of wine to North Devon is documented by imports into Barnstaple between 1383 and 1389 (Duffy et al. 1992, 62-63; 66). A document in the Cornish record office details the shipping of wine from Appledore in 1393/4 (CRO AR/2/539/5). At the beginning of the 16th century Youings and Cornford estimate the North Devon ports were importing c.75 tuns of wine a year (1992, 102). Fisher notes that c.1720 Barnstaple was importing more wine than Bideford and also documents trade with the American colonies (1992, 235).

An unusual import into Devon is represented by a seal found in topsoil during North Devon Archaeological Society evaluation trenches at Higher Holworthy (Plate 10.8). The seal is worn and the first word is unclear but enhanced digitally appears to read 'HERMITAGIE'. The second word is 'WYN' (Dutch wijn) and the type is closely paralleled by Dutch/Belgian long necked bottles dating to the latter part of the eighteenth century. Examples of a wine named after the wife of a Dutch Governor in South Africa, 'CONSTANTIA WYN', are noted in Ruggles-Brise (1949, 93). Other known examples of similar type are sealed 'CLARET' or 'BOERGONIE' / 'BOURGOGNE WYN' (Burgundy wine) so it has been suggested that the Holworthy seal may read 'Hermitage wine' in English (Polly Thompson, pers. comm.).

This example is exceptional however; most sealed bottles found in North Devon were for local people and would presumably have been made within a reasonable radius. The proximity of ports may partly explain the high proportion of sealed bottles in this part of the county but the prime driver behind demand for these symbols of self-esteem must have been fashion.

ACKNOWLEDGEMENTS

I would like to thank the staff of the museums involved, in particular Alison Mills and Ruth Spires (Museum of Barnstaple and North Devon), Sue Scrutton (Torrington Museum), Jenny Yendall (South Molton and District Museum) and Liz Curtis (Holsworthy Museum) for their assistance with recording. (A comprehensive digital record of all North Devon seals has been placed with each of the aforementioned museums.)

I am indebted to Stephen Hobbs for help with the Luttrell family and to his wife Liz for help with Dutch translation. James Coulter was invaluable in providing information concerning the genealogy of the Rolles and Bourchier Wreys. Thanks too to Terry Green who brought the Dutch/Belgian seal to my attention and to Kevin Shaddick for showing me his collection.

11
Arlington Court, Devon

An archaeological survey of the estate for the National Trust

Nick Berry

Introduction and background

Arlington Court lies at the centre of the National Trust's Arlington estate in North Devon. Situated approximately seven kilometres northeast of Barnstaple and an equivalent distance south-southeast of Combe Martin, the estate extends to 1404.5 hectares (3471 acres). Arlington was generously bequeathed to the Trust by Miss Rosalie Chichester in 1949, the last of the Chichester family to live at Arlington.

The estate encompasses the gently sloping plateau of Arlington itself and the similar topography of Arlington Beccott to the north set within higher ground in every direction. Beyond to the south the ground rises to an east-west ridge cut through by the River Yeo, then falls steadily to Loxhore. All the streams are tributaries of the River Yeo that runs through the estate from north to south. The land use can be divided into the historic core of ornamental gardens and parkland around Arlington Court, extensive woodland and plantations, and enclosed farmland. There are currently nine farms on the estate with other land farmed in-hand by the National Trust.

Arlington Court is a Grade II★ listed mansion built in two phases, the first in 1820-23. The first phase was "an austere, even stark, essay in the Greek Revival" (Cornforth, 1981: 1179) forming a relatively small rectangular block. The only outward decoration is the entrance on the east framed by a semi-circular Doric porch of fluted columns. The extension to the north was built in the 1860s and has an almost institutional appearance in contrast to the earlier building (Plate 11.1). An attractive colonnaded extension to the stable block was built at the same time.

The building of the mansion was complemented by a transformation of the surrounding landscape into formal gardens and extensive parkland. It was a transformation achieved over a relatively short period of time, and almost regardless of cost. However, the ambition of its vision, and the near total dominance of the effects, has tended to blind the visitor to the earlier history of Arlington. But there is a fascinating earlier history.

Previous archaeological work and documentary sources

Elements of the older Arlington have been identified by previous archaeological work over a number of years, notably by the work of Colin Humphreys and Terry Green

(1996, 1998, 1999[2007]). These efforts have concentrated in the formal gardens and the Wilderness combe, including excavations of the dam of the lower pond, and a survey of the Wilderness. A small excavation was undertaken in the paddock south of the church in 1998 where there are significant earthworks of formal garden terraces associated with the earlier houses of the Chichester family.

Documentary evidence in the form of an estate map from 1776 by Charles Hassall shows a small manor house located immediately south of the church. The building is the centre of a small community of cottages and possibly the odd farmhouse south and southwest of the manor house. These buildings were subsequently removed and contemporary paintings by Maria Pixcel show a grander three storey mansion built around 1790, complemented by a new Picturesque landscape (Plate 11.2). The new house was also located south of the church but the exact location was not clear until recently. Fortunately, earlier this year, the National Trust House Steward David Gibbons discovered copies of the original plans for the three storey mansion, and plans and elevation drawings of the earlier manor house. These clearly demonstrate that not only was the 1790 house built on the earlier one in the same place, but the earlier house was also constructed around an identifiable medieval core. The origins of this house certainly pre-date the arrival of the Chichester family at Arlington in 1534, although they had held the property since 1385. The property had previously been held by another north Devon family, the Raleghs, for over 200 years.

The recent survey

Between December 2007 and May 2008 an extensive survey of the Arlington landscape was carried out. Every field and patch of woodland was visited and archaeological sites and features were identified and plotted on 1:2500 scale maps. Gradually, elements of the older landscape emerged from the nineteenth century parkland, but the sheer scale of the Chichesters' ambition in the nineteenth century was also revealed. The details cannot all be related here, so we will concentrate on a

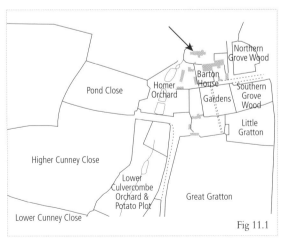

Fig 11.1

few main findings from the survey that shed some light on the main periods of change and development at the centre of the estate.

SURVEY RESULTS
Prehistory
The first factor to note is that Arlington is a prime location for human settlement. The location at the head of the (Wilderness) combe, with a small tributary stream of the Yeo would almost certainly have been visited by Mesolithic hunter-gatherer groups. There is no direct evidence to support this assertion in the shape of lithic scatters or stray finds, but the location is a classic site, although much altered by later changes and landscaping. One significant find from the estate is a piece of polished Neolithic axe from Langdale in the Lake District, but much altered and reworked, found behind the Old Post Office on the A39 (Fox, 1955: 319-320).

The topographical characteristics of the location also give it several advantages for agricultural settlement. Arlington has relatively large areas (for north Devon) of reasonably level land for plough agriculture, and good access to higher ground for pasture and rough grazing to the east. Sheltered from the north the location of early settlement around the head of the combe or nearby is highly likely. We should expect the location to be permanently settled by later prehistory. The pattern of known late prehistoric enclosures in this part of north Devon shows a gap in the Arlington area, even if the probable Romano-British enclosure along Lock Lane to the east is included. The survey identified a route of probable prehistoric origins running west down the centre of the spur from the high ground to the east. A continuation of this alignment takes it to the centre of the medieval settlement next to the church, and it is likely that this route continued in use until the post-medieval period or beyond.

Medieval settlement and deer park
That Arlington was a prime location is perhaps supported by the size of the Domesday

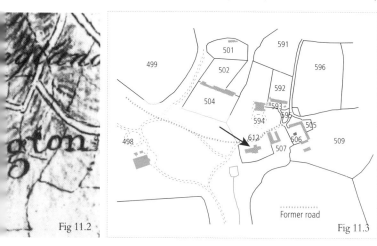

Fig 11.2

Former road

Fig 11.3

Fig 11
Sixty years that changed the Arlington landscape. The only constant is the church (arrowed).
Fig 11.1 1776
Fig 11.2 1805
Fig 11.3 1840
(11.2 OS Surveyor's Draft: Courtesy West Country Studies Library)

59

manor. In Shirwell hundred there were 42 manors, only one of which was taxed for two hides and five for one hide, one of which was Arlington. So although small by the standards of the rest of Devon, the manor was above average for north Devon. The Domesday record of 1086 lists one Alvred de Ispania as holding Arlington or Alferdinton as the name was then recorded. Alvred may have been a Spanish mercenary employed by the Conqueror. The neighbouring manor of Tuchel or Twitchen was added to the holding, and together these landholdings may have been roughly equivalent to the current parish of Arlington. Survivals from this early period include in part the pattern of field boundaries that fossilise medieval ploughlands at New England, and hints of ridge and furrow in the western park at Arlington. Unfortunately these could not be clarified by available aerial photographs. Given the surviving extent of medieval fields at Arlington Beccott and the noted separation of the lord's demesne and peasants' land in Devon (Victoria County History, 1906: 384), it is likely that Arlington Beccott was the latter, a subordinate settlement.

There are good documentary sources that show the descent of the manor in the Ralegh family (Reichel, 1935), which by the 1340s was growing in wealth and influence. A succession of documents from the 1340s includes a Charter of Feoffment by John de Lokkeshore to Thomas de Raleghe of land to be enclosed by a new ditch (DRO 50/11/22/2-4). It becomes clear that the ditch is the boundary of a new park, including Wytemorewode, and becomes the new deer park for the estate. The land is taken from the parish of Loxhore and Wytemorewode is now Deer Park Wood. Many of the substantial boundary banks of this park have been identified on the ground by

Plate 11.2:
The 1790 house
south of the church.
Contemporary
painting by Maria
Pixcel.
(National Trust
Archive)

this and earlier survey work (my thanks to Colin Humphreys), although the complete bounds require an element of interpretation.

The survey identified a number of other features from this period including several large holloways running down through Woolley Wood and Deer Park Wood, including in the latter a track that has clearly been truncated by the 1340s deer park boundary, therefore pre-dating it. These are just parts of a wider network of communication that would have linked Arlington with Loxhore and Shirwell, or simply routes from farmland onto unenclosed heathland. Most of these are incomplete or interrupted by development of the later parkland.

Post-medieval expansion

Arlington would seem to have grown slowly, unspectacularly, with the Chichester family making no great impact after the property came to them through marriage in 1385. Arlington seems to have been leased and managed by stewards and agents for 150 years. In 1534 Amyas Chichester became the first member of the family to live at Arlington and is recorded as enlarging the old medieval manor house. But clearly the family had not been idle and their estates had grown. The reason we know this is the punishment of the family for recusancy in 1608. The Chichester family were Catholics and had consistently refused to attend Protestant services. Their punishment was the loss of two thirds of the estate for 41 years, but the details of the charges list landholdings much enlarged since the Domesday survey of five hundred years earlier (DRO 50/11/2/3). This is also a key period in the development of the estate.

In 1630 the high ground to the east known as Arlington Down, was enclosed. Many of the boundaries from this process survive, and although unspectacular, represent a symbolic break with the medieval past to a more modern agricultural world. It is likely the development was prompted by the increased demands and expansion of Barnstaple, and by the challenge of a growing agrarian capitalism. Many leases from this period give the former commoners 16-18 acres 'in lieu of commons', but it would have been the Chichester family who ultimately benefited. The village of Arlington Beccott also demonstrates elements of contemporary planning in the layout of its farms (Isabel Richardson, pers. comm.).

The Chichesters were land managers. They did not own overseas plantations, were not involved in shipping or other trade as far as we can tell, but managed their own patch of North Devon for generations. They continued to suffer persecution as Catholics in a strongly Protestant country, but a succession of good marriages in the later seventeenth and eighteenth centuries provided them with an increased income and better prospects. It was also a period in which those with land prospered, while those without lost position. Despite their faith, the Chichesters were on the right side of the equation, or more particularly, the growing social divisions.

At this period the centre of the estate had been gradually developed. The old medieval and Tudor manor house had been given a formal Palladian façade, probably in the early eighteenth century, and some of the messier farming activities may have been allocated to Beccott to gentrify the core of the estate at Arlington itself (Isabel Richardson pers. comm.). Lost carriage driveways from this period were identified by the survey in the park and woodland, as were some remnants of formal planting. But Arlington remained stubbornly small scale. More significant changes were needed to create the landscape we know today.

A new house and 'picturesque' landscape

These changes seem to coincide with the succession to the estate of Colonel John Palmer Chichester (1769-1823). Sadly the Colonel's first wife, Mary Ann Cary died a few days after giving birth to their only child in 1791. The Colonel's second wife was Mary Hamilton of Bangour in Scotland, and in a monumental break with family faith and tradition, she was a Protestant. The Colonel recanted his faith at Exeter Cathedral in 1793, and at Arlington 'the oldest chaplaincy in Devon was closed up, and the last incumbent, the Reverend Henry Innes, was turned adrift' (Oliver, 1857, quoted in the National Trust handbook, 1985: 32).

The Colonel initiated other major changes. By 1790 a grand three-storey house designed by John Meadows had been built around the core of the much adapted medieval house. The old medieval fishponds in Culvercombe orchard were remodelled as ornamental features. A new 'picturesque' landscape was created, recorded in contemporary paintings by Maria Pixcel, with the orchards in Culvercombe removed to create a fashionable Wilderness with new plantations and cascades in the stream. The creation of this new landscape would have necessitated the removal of the cottages and outbuildings shown close to the 'barton' on the Hassall map of 1776. There is no documentary record of the process or what happened to the tenants, though some faint earthworks survive. The later 1805 OS draft map also shows further buildings to the north and west of the church, the area not covered by the Charles Hassall survey (Fig. 11.1). There is no doubt that Arlington was a small village or hamlet, the main settlement in the parish, in the documents often referred to as Arlington Church Town.

The 1790 house did not last. Local tradition suggests it was so badly built that it had to be pulled down, but perhaps more likely it was simply in the wrong place. The position close by the church was cramped and prevented full expression both for the house and surrounding parkland landscape. A new site was to found. A large level platform in the park west of the Wilderness has been known for some years, and it would seem to have been the initial choice of site prepared for the Colonel's new house. However, it is rather exposed, and has a relatively short view over level parkland to the south, so a new site was chosen, that of the current Arlington Court.

The second new house and enlarged parkland

The new house designed by Thomas Lee from Barnstaple was finished in 1823, the year that Colonel Chichester died. The new house shifted the focus of the parkland west of the Wilderness combe and completed a massive expansion of the parkland to west and south commenced in the previous phase. However it also meant the removal of the buildings west of the church shown on the 1805 OS map. These would now lie in the garden somewhere between the church and current house (Fig. 11.1). In December 2007 a small watching brief identified a compacted lime mortar floor during removal of diseased rhododendrons on the front lawn. Again the family documentary record is silent.

However, the population census from the period 1801-1821 does show a marked reduction in houses, families and number of individuals in the parish at a time when the general population was increasing dramatically, and there were increases in all categories in all the neighbouring parishes. It would seem there was a social cost to Colonel Chichester's ambitions, but what happened to the tenants is unknown. We would expect them to be re-housed elsewhere on the estate, but this requires further research.

The expansion and development of the parkland was continued by the Colonel's son, Sir John Palmer Bruce Chichester (1794-1851). After a distinguished naval career Sir John became MP for Barnstaple, and Arlington was developed as an estate to match his new status and ambition. The road through the old Arlington hamlet was blocked and lodges built at the entrances. The main road (from Shirwell to Kentisbury) was also blocked and rebuilt on a longer, winding route (the current A39). These developments may have made the family unpopular with some local people, but would also have provided a great deal of work. The parkland was greatly expanded. Miles of superbly engineered carriage driveways were constructed, no doubt employing professional surveyors, and many new park boundaries were faced with 'Jack and Jill' stonework.

No great park could be complete without a lake, and Sir John had the River Yeo dammed to create one by 1840. However this was soon deemed too small and he had plans to enlarge it further and build a suspension bridge across it as the climax of the network of carriage driveways around the estate. The bridge piers were built, and the lake was extended 200m and dammed again (the current dam). But the project was abandoned in the 1850s, leaving the bridge piers still standing. By this time his son Sir Alexander Palmer Bruce Chichester had inherited the property, and although already in debt, continued to spend heavily, enlarging the mansion in the 1860s. Continual changes and refinements were made to the parkland and ever increasing network of carriage driveways. Most are still used, but some have been lost or survive as shallow earthworks across outlying fields. Except for the detail changes it is this landscape that dominates the visitor perception of Arlington today. But it is a relatively recent phenomenon. Arlington hides its age very well.

Further away from the centre of the estate the older landscape resurfaces, but even here there are elements of formal planting located in the farmland and along approach roads. The road from Loxhore Cott was widened for one and half kilometres south to Loxhore Bridge. The southern end may even have been constructed anew to provide the southern entrance to the estate with a suitable approach.

Other points of interest

Other findings from the survey include the tentative interpretation of three possible prehistoric enclosures: two at Loxhore and one at North Woolley. All are fragmentary and inconclusive and require further study, but the locations are potentially significant. There are also extensive survivals of medieval field boundaries at Loxhore, not just as existing curving hedgebanks but also as flattened ridge and furrow and substantial earthworks. The field southeast of the church contains a large number of earthworks of field boundaries and platforms of former buildings, suggesting Loxhore is a shrunken village. At Churchill the field pattern also reveals elements of medieval strip fields in the boundary pattern.

The documentary evidence provides clues about a lost chapel or priory at Churchill referred to by Richard Polwhele (1977: 399). A charter of 1130 grants a *ferling at Churchill as free from all dues* to the monks of St. Martin des Champs at Barnstaple (Reichel, 1935: 417-8). But it cannot be this grant that is the origin of the place-name as Churchill was known as Cercilla in the Domesday survey of 1086. Was there an even older religious establishment at Churchill? Later documentary sources, for example from 1675, 1704 and 1764 refer to a small piece of land called "St. Martin's Chapell and Chappell Hey" but unfortunately the field names do not survive to the tithe apportionment. Further research is required to identify the location. As is usual with this work it can raise more questions than it answers.

One other group of remains are worth mentioning as they took considerable time to map. These are leats, or catch meadow systems designed to irrigate pasture and meadowland. The estate is full of them, and some run for hundreds of yards along the contour, although one exception, at Loxhore Cott, covers a whole meadow with swirling channels. It is almost a work of art in itself., but very time consuming to record. Most date from the late seventeenth to nineteenth century, and are now disused. But they are useful for relative dating purposes as they often cut or are cut by other features.

12
A Harvest of Jugs

Alison Mills

In September 2008, the Museum of Barnstaple and North Devon put together an exhibition of North Devon Harvest Jugs. The temporary closure of the Royal Albert Memorial Museum , Exeter, for refurbishment, offered the opportunity to bring 14 jugs back to North Devon, and together with further pieces from the Burton Art Gallery and Museum, Bideford, and the museum's own collections, we were able to present the most comprehensive group of jugs ever assembled in one exhibition.

North Devon post-mediaeval sgraffito pottery is a common find in gardens and excavations throughout the South West of England and is found as far afield as Ireland and the New World. Production at the kilns of Barnstaple and Bideford reached its peak during the second half of the 17th century. Typically the potters made wide-rimmed dishes of Fremington clay, coated them with Petersmarland clay slip and scratched through a geometric or naturally-inspired design before firing and glazing.

The increasing availability of good-quality tablewares from Bristol and Staffordshire from the 18th century onwards led North Devon potters to concentrate almost exclusively on the plain pitchers, bowls and storage jars which were their stock in trade well into the 20th century. However, the decorated sgraffito jug managed to maintain its place in local households, and the North Devon Harvest Jug tradition continues unbroken to the present day.

The exhibition "A Harvest of Jugs", which ran from September 6th to November 8th 2008, brought together 29 jugs dating from 1703 to 1998. This article offers the opportunity to describe their decoration, rhymes and where possible maker, together with their museum accession numbers, and we hope will be a useful reference for readers with an interest in these beautiful and evocative North Devon products.

Further Reading

Grant, Alison, *North Devon Pottery, the Seventeenth Century*, University of Exeter, 1983
Grant, Alison, *North Devon Pottery*, Edward Gaskell, 2005
Edgeler, John, *The Fishleys of Fremington, A Devon Slipware Tradition*, Cotswold Living Publications, 2008
Holland, William Fishley, *Fifty Years a Potter*, Pottery Quarterly, 1958
Brears, Peter, *The Collectors Book of English Country Pottery*, David & Charles, 1974

Early Jugs

The Exeter Hare and Hounds jug, dated 1703, is one of the earliest surviving harvest jugs. Similar in style is a jug in the Firzwilliam Museum, Cambridge, which is dated 1703/4. In both jugs, the rhyme is inscribed right around the pot, rather than in a panel as in later examples.

Jug 1 RAMM 233/1978

Jug 8 RAMM 74/1931/2

Jug 9 RAMM 218/1982

Jug 13 RAMM 76/1927/4

66

Jug 6 BAGM 1192.527

Harvest or celebration?
Although commonly known as harvest jugs, these sgraffito jugs were made to commemorate a range of family and national events, including the Act of Union and the Napoleonic Wars. Maritime motifs are also common, including mermaids and sea monsters as well as ships and compasses.

Jug 18 MBND
(Tawstock Loan)

Jug 12 BAGM 1992.500

Jug 16 RAMM 146/1982

18th century potters

This group of jugs, clearly by the same potter, have sometimes been attributed to John Phillips, whose name appears on the inscription of the Museum of Barnstaple and North Devon jug. However, the maker is more likely to be Thomas Fields of Bideford, who inscribed his name on the handle. A fifth jug, in the collections of the British Museum can also be attributed to the same maker.

Jug 2 MBND 1931.1397

Jug 5 RAMM 38/1930

Jug 3 RAMM 64/1929

Jug 4 RAMM 83/1929

The Fishley Family

The Fishley family of Fremington were largely responsible for the survival of the harvest jug tradition in North Devon. George Fishley (1770-1869) moved from Bideford to Fremington in 1800. His sons Edmund (1806-1860) and Robert (1808-1887) and grandson Edwin Beer continued the tradition.

Jug 11 BAGM 1992.271

Jug 17 MBND 2005.76   Jug 23 MBND 1992.2007   Jug 14 RAMM 369/1977

Later jugs

Edwin Beer Fishley (1832-1912) continued making harvest jugs at Fremington in particular producing many fairly standardised jugs towards the end of the 19th century. He shared his skills with the Barnstaple Art Potters C.H.Brannam and William Baron, and trained his grandson William Fishley Holland, who later became a studio potter at Clevedon. Harry Juniper is still making traditional North Devon jugs in Bideford.

Jug 29 MBND 2009.39

Jug 27 MBND 1994.225.12

Jug 26 RAMM 119/1997

Jug 20 RAMM 76/1927/5

Catalogue of exhibited jugs

RAMM - Royal Albert Memorial Museum. Exter
BAGM - Burton Art Gellery & Museum Bideford
MBND - Museum of Barnstaple & North Devon

Jug 1
Hare chased by hounds and hunter
1703 Maker - unknown

MPM 1703

*The fearfull hare doth run a pace; because
the hounds are on thare chace; the country
hee is forst to fly ; whilst they pursue with
hue and cry; nature hath taught him in this
stile to seek for to presarve his life; which hee
by running doth obtaine; and then the
hounds return againe; The huntsman seeing
that doth cry; Lett him goe his meat is dry;
Ile to my landladee with speed; for I of her
have greater need.*

RAMM 233/1978

Jug 2
John Phillips Jug, royal coat of arms,
mermaids, monsters
1760 Thomas Fields, Bideford

*When I was in my native place/I was a
lumpe of clay/And Digged up out of the
earth .And brought from thens away/But
now a jug I am become/By potters art and
skill/And I your servant am became/And
Carie Ale I will. John Phillips 1760*

MBND (North Devon Athenaeum)
1991.1397

Jug 3
Compass, ship, mermaid, sea monster.
1766 ?Thomas Fields, Bideford

*Come fill me full and Drinke aboute/and
never leave till all is out/And if that will
not make you merry/Fill me again and sing
Down Derry 1766*

RAMM 64/1929

Jug 4
Compass motif with flower in centre,
mermaid, flatfish, bird, waves; sailing ship,
sea monster, waves, chevron border
1771 ?Thomas Fields, Bideford

*Work on Brave Boys and never fear/You
shall have ale, cyder and beer/But pork and
pudding as I think/I rear good eating with
Strong Drinke 1771*

RAMM 83/1929

Jug 5
Royal coat of arms
1775 ?Thomas Fields, Bideford

*Harvis is come all bissy now/in mackin of
your Barly mow when men do laber hard
and swet/Good ale is better far than meet
Bideford April 28 1775 M+W*

RAMM 38/1930

Jug 6
Goddess Ceres, wheatsheafs, birds in
flowering branches
1795 Unknown

*When I was in my native place I was a
lump of clay/and digged up out of the earth
and brought from thance away/But now a
pot i am become by potters art and skill/and
now your servant am become and carry ale I
will/Jovial fellows drink about we'll have
more when this is out. Mr Jn Fisher Court
Bartin Yarnscombe/1795*

BAGM 1992.527

Jug 7 (not illustrated)
Birds on flowering plants.
1798 Unknown

*When this you see/pray think on me/And
think me not unkind/Let all the world say
what they will/Speak of me as you find.
The King is crowned that has no end/So is
my love unto my friend William and Mary
Toowle May the 9 1798/E G*

RAMM 46/1930

Jug 8
Crowned lion and flowering plants
1818 John Bird Bideford

*August 25 1818/Drink round my jovial
fellow and when that this is done/We'll
have the other jug my boys/and sing a
merry song Wm Ough Quathiock/made by
Jn Bird Potter Bideford*

RAMM 74/1931/2

Jug 9
Flowering plants
1830 Unknown

*1830/James Charles/Despise me not
because I'm Made of clay/but make me
welcomw when I comethis way/My belly fill
with good strong punh or beer/and I will
make you merry all the year*

RAMM 218/1982

Jug 10 (not illustrated)
Flowering plants.
1830-1860 Unknown, probably Bideford

No inscription

RAMM 68/1928

Jug 11
Butterflies, tulips and a cockerel
1837 Robert Fishley, Fremington

*The tulip and the butterfly Appear in gayer
coats than I Let me be dressed fine as I will
Flies worms and flowers exceed me still
Henry Shambrook, Bideford, June 22nd
1837*

BAGM 1992.271

Jug 12
Modelled figure of Nelson on spout,
white ensign and French flag, bird on
plant
1830-1860 ?George Fishley, Fremington
BAGM 1992.500

Jug 13
Tulip, butterfly, wheatear, jug, goblet.
1839 Edmund Fishley, Fremington

*Wm Mildon Halswell Chittlehampton
1839 The tulip and the butterfly/Appear in
gayer coats than I/Long may you
live/Happy may you be/Blest with
content/and from misfortuns free/This little
jug in friendship take and keep it for the
giver's sake/Rebecca Searle June 6th 1839
Edmund Fishley maker Fremington*

RAMM 76/1927/4

Jug 14
Three flags of the union and shamrock,
rose, thistle below birds, a fruiting vine,
jug, pipe and glass, butterfly, wheat ears.
1839 George Fishley, Fremington

*The Rose and the thistle and shamrock so
green/England, Irelan, Scotland and
Wales/Peace plenty and hapynis reign in
your vales/M S Fisher's jug
Hunshaw/November 5 1839
Long may you live/Happy may you
be/Blest with content/and from misfortune
free
George Fishley/Maker Fremington*

RAMM 369/1977

Jug 15 (not illustrated)
Ploughing scene and portrait of John
Wesley.
1840–1860 Robert Fishley, Fremington

*He that by the plough would thrive Himself
must either hold or drive* (On handle)
March 8th R Fishley jug

RAMM 100/1930

Jug 16
Ship, flowering plants, fish.
1840–1870 ?Barnstaple

No inscription

RAMM 146/1982

Jug 17
Moths, cockerel, tulips and more
1847 "Robert Fishley, Fremington"

*Mary Cooper Sept 28th 1847/Robert
Fishley Maker Fremington pottery*

MBND 2005.76

Jug 18
Tawstock Ringers' Jug, bells
1850 Edmund Fishley, Fremington

*1812 Success to the hearty ringers of
Tawstock/The youngest ringers shall carry
the jug/E.Fishley Fremington 1850*

MBND Tawstock PCC Loan

Jug 19 (not illustrated)
Leaf resist and sgraffito birds on branches
1856 Unknown, probably Fremington

*Emmanuel Wyburn 1856 Long may you
live/happy may you be/Blest with
content/And from misfortune Free*

MBND 1991.856

Jug 20
Flowering plants, birds, sunburst.
1861 Unknown, ?Bideford

*Long may we Live/Happy may we
be/Blest with content/and from misfortunes
free/Mary Palmer January 2nd 1861*

RAMM 76/1927/5

Jug 21 (not illustrated)
Flowering plants, birds, flowerpot contains
the inscription.
1866 Bideford

*Miss Ann Williams/ Paul may plant/ and
Appolos water/ but God gives/ Me increase
Bideford/1866*

RAMM 74/1931/1

Jug 22a and Jug 22b (not illustrated)
Pair of jugs, inscriptions enclosed by
wreaths with plants and wheatsheaves.
The jugs mark the union of two farming
families.
1868 E.B.Fishley Fremington

*Good luck to the hoof and the horn/Good
luck to the flock and the fleece/Good luck to
the growers of corn/May we always have
plenty and peace See harvest comes with
yellow glory crown/While lads and lasses
make the hills resound/The farmer's heart is
likewise full of glee/To reap the fruits of
their Industry/E.B.Fishley Potter
Fremington*

(Jug 22a John Squire/1868/Swimbridge,
Jug 22b John Irwin/1868/Chittlehampton)
MBND loan, private collection

Jug 23
Inscription enclosed by wheatears,
cannon and crossed rifles.
1871 E.B.Fishley, Fremington

*Long may you live/happy may you
be/Blest with content/And from misfortune
Free Success to the farmer the plough and
the flail/Likewise to our commerce/With
Peace in our lives/1871/Josiah Bentley
Baker, Enfield*

MBND 1992.2077

Jug 24 (not illustrated)
Inscription enclosed by wreath, touches
of coloured glaze
1876 E.B.Fishley, Fremington

*Success to the farmer/The plough and the
flail/May the landlord ever flourish/And
the tenant never fail. Long may you
live/Happy may you be/Blest with
content/And from misfortune free John
Dullam, Hele, Tawstock, 1876/This jug in
friendship take/and keep it for Grace
Bubb's sake*

MBND loan, private collection

Jug 25 (not illustrated)
Viking ships. Owen Davies, a successful
London designer, also designed pots by
C.H.Brannam in 1879.
1879 E.B.Fishley and Owen Davies,
Fremington

No inscription

MBND 1992.1391

Jug 26
Sunburst. Signed Brannam
c. 1879 CH Brannam, Barnstaple

Monogram ?OHD

RAMM 119/1997

Jug 27
1881 E.B.Fishley, Fremington

*Success to the farmer/ the plough and the
flail/May the landlord ever flourich/And
the tenant never fail Good luck to the hoof
and the horn/Good luck to the flock and
the fleece/Good luck to the growers of
corn/May we ever have plenty and peace
John N Miller, Raleigh House*

MBND NDA 1994.225.12

Jug 28 (not illustrated)
Coat of arms, railway scenes
1994 Harry Juniper, Bideford

Lynton & Barnstaple Railway 1898-1935

MBND 1996.5

Jug 29
Barnstaple landmarks, including Queen
Anne's Walk, Clock Tower, Butchers Row
1998 Harry Juniper, Bideford

*World in Bloom/won by/Barnstaple/the
Pearl of Devon/1998*

MBND 2009.39

13
Going to Town

Terry Green

We think we know what a town is: a place with streets and shops and a lot of people. So why do we find small, out of the way rural places, perhaps single farms called 'Town'? Isn't that inappropriate? Here we shall look at some of these in North Devon and consider what the term might mean and what historical significance it might have.

Our present understanding of the word town, ie. a conurbation, dates from the Middle English period, say 13th-15th century. The word descends from the Common Germanic *tūn*, which in German becomes *Zaun* (fence) and in Dutch *tuin* (garden) and originally meant a fence or hedge. Among the Angles and Saxons in England it developed a variety of meanings all ultimately derived from the idea of a fenced or hedged enclosure, so that we find, for example, *æppeltūn* (orchard), *lēactūn* (vegetable garden), *līctūn* (graveyard). From 'an enclosed piece of ground' the word comes to signify an enclosure with a dwelling and thus a farmstead, a hamlet, a larger community. It also develops into a term for manor or estate and as such comes to designate a major 'central place' and the land belonging to it (Smith, 1970)); in North Devon Braunton, Tawton, Torrington, Molton and Harton (Hartland) are examples. In the later pre-Conquest period the use of the term proliferated as land became more and more developed or divided up, leading to the huge number of -ton place names that litter the British landscape. Although very many of the places called 'something-ton' are now villages, towns or cities, they very probably were all individual farmsteads in the first place.

'Town' meaning 'farm' is retained in Scottish dialect, but is otherwise no longer current in English. However, there is a vestige of this usage in the term 'Barton' which is so frequently encountered in the nomenclature of the Devon landscape. The word 'barton' originates from Old English *beretūn*, meaning literally 'grain-farm' which suggests a settlement on good arable land and may belong originally to the ancient system of 'multiple estates' in which land was apparently designated for specific uses, in this case for the growing of cereals. The importance of wheat, barley and rye as staple foods implies that a 'barton' must be important, and in fact when we encounter the term in post-medieval records it is very frequently attached to a farm adjacent to the church and the manor house or perhaps to the manor house itself. And quite often in this context we find the historically tautological Barton Town or Town Barton.

In addition to Barton Town (or Town Barton) we also encounter Church Town and

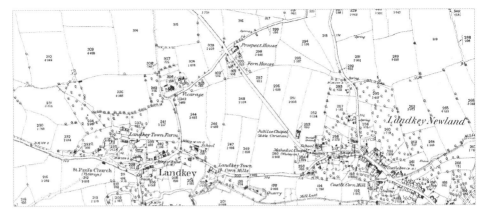

Fig.13.1:
Extract from the
Ordnance Survey
First Edition map at
1:2500, published
1889, showing
Landkey Town to
the west and
Landkey Newland
to the east.

in some cases (place-name) + Town, for example Landkey Town. In fact Landkey is a good place to start looking into the potential significance of 'Towns' in the landscape. It is generally accepted that the name Landkey is one of rather few surviving British-Celtic names in Devon, representing the 'lan' or sacred enclosure of St Kea, a Celtic saint. It is therefore a very early name. Figure 13.1 is an extract from the OS First Edition 1:2500 map showing the two elements of Landkey. To the east is Landkey Newland and to the west Landkey Town with the church and Town Farm which, on later OS maps is graced with the words - in Gothic type -'Old Manor'. We must assume that Newland means what it says, and that what is now the major part of the village was at some date a new development along the line of the road from Barnstaple to Swimbridge at a certain distance from Landkey Town. The fact that the church and the 'Old Manor' or Town Farm lie side by side in Landkey Town strongly suggests that this is the location of the medieval manorial demesne farm out of which the settlement grew. The juxtaposition of parish church and manor house and/or principal farm is a pattern that we see repeated again and again throughout Devon and well beyond. While in the case of Landkey it is possible that the church or a chapel came first, in most cases it is thought that the location was first chosen for its agricultural and other practical virtues and that the church followed when the lord of the manor decided it was time he or his people should have one (see Morris 1989, 140-167). Landkey therefore, displays a pattern of settlement shift away from the original manorial centre which remains detectable through its significant features and with which the term 'Town' has become associated.

Having laid the ground with Landkey, let us look at Parracombe. Here we find the core of the village today lying in the valley where Ley's Lane crosses the River Heddon. Here are Parracombe Mill and, standing only a couple of hundred metres from the village centre, Holwell Castle, a very well preserved Norman motte and bailey whose location here is a mystery. The parish contains three Domesday manors and a number of hamlets lying within a landscape that aerial photography has shown to be marked by extensive areas of medieval strip lynchets. On the rising ground to the east of the village and about a kilometre from the present heart of the village and

74

the Victorian parish church is Parracombe Church Town with the church of St Petrock and Court Place, the manor house of Parracombe. Beside the churchyard is a house called Barton from which leads Barton Lane. To the north of the church is the glebe and what was formerly the rectory. Of the three Domesday manors, named Parracombe, Middleton and Rowley, Parracombe was the largest (Thorn and Thorn 1985). Parracombe Church Town thus has all the signs of being the early focus of settlement, while what is now thought of as the village of Parracombe has grown up relatively recently around the river crossing and Parracombe Mill. This is therefore another case of settlement shift or at least of a transposed centre of growth.

Similarly if we look at the neighbouring parish of Challacombe, we find Barton Town set at some distance from what passes today as the village of Challacombe which lies beside the B3358 road. Barton Town consists of the parish church and a farm. The parish of Challacombe is large and contains a number of hamlets among which are Whitefield and Wallover with their own bartons, Buscombe and the now abandoned Radworthy all of which together with Challacombe itself were small Domesday manors, among which Challacombe held the highest valuation in 1086 (Thorn and Thorn 1985). As in the case of Parracombe, aerial survey has revealed evidence of widespread medieval strip lynchets in the parish especially around Whitefield, Swincombe (not a Domesday manor) and Barton Town. Although at present settlement is concentrated along the B3358 road, inspection of the topography of the ground adjacent to the parish church (Plate 13.1) suggests that Barton Town represents the remnant of a formerly larger settlement. Although there is a 'Town Farm' within the modern settlement group on the main road, the combination of church, farm and settlement cluster with the name Barton Town suggests that this was the original medieval heart of the parish. An additional consideration is that what is probably a drove or stock-track leads almost directly from here to the edge of the open moor, skirting round the concentrated area of strip lynchets associated with Swincombe.

Moving westwards to the Holsworthy area, the village of Clawton presents an interesting case. Clawton is a small settlement in West Devon District. Today Clawton

Plate 13.1: Barton Town Challacombe with 'humps and bumps' in the foreground. (Photo: T. Green)

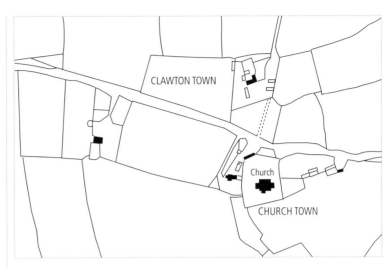

Fig.13.2:
Tracing from the
Clawton tithe
map of 1844.

presents principally a cluster of dwellings with post office and primary school situated beside Clawton Bridge roughly 5 kilometres due south of Holsworthy on the Holsworthy to Launceston A388 road. Half a kilometre from Clawton Bridge the church of St Leonard stands on a spur overlooking the River Claw. To the west of the church is the Vicarage and next along the road is Court Barn, now a hotel, but originally a private residence *possibly* descended from the manor house of Clawton. To the north on the other side of the east-west road is Town Farm. On the First Edition Ordnance Survey maps of around 1890 this is named Church Town, while on the tithe map of 1844 it is Clawton Town. The tithe map places Church Town to the south of the road, where at that date there was a cottage and a pair of barns (Fig. 13.2). In fact study of the records indicates a long-term vacillation between the names Church Town and Clawton Town, a confusion which appears to have its origin in an amalgamation of two separate holdings in the late 18th century, one on either side of the road.

The manorial history of Clawton is itself confused, the manor having frequently changed hands. The most sustained period of ownership was that of the Chudleigh family who acquired the manor in 1325 and whose line held it until the 16th century. According to Lysons (1822), by 1620 the lord of the manor of Clawton was John Allyn. This gentleman's grave slab is to be seen in the chancel of the parish church bearing an inscription that tells us that he was 'of the Church Town' (Plate 13.2). While it has been thought that Court Barton to the west of the church might represent the ancient manor house, it appears from the information on the grave slab that the lord of the manor in the early 17th century resided at Church Town, and according to the tithe map this was to the east of the church. All that stands here now is an L-shaped barn, one wing of which probably remains from the period of the tithe survey. However between the barn and the churchyard and extending to the south the topography suggests building platforms, terraces and trackways. This is where the local historian Harvey (1939, 30) states that the remains of a holding named Church Town are to be seen and it is also where the tithe map of 1844 has a field named 'Garden'. It is also where elaborate architectural fragments have been found propped against a hedge bank, perhaps relics of a demolished manor house.

At Clawton then, we have another example of the Town by the church with signs of an abandoned or shrunken settlement, the existing settlement having relocated to a position on the nearby main road. It is interesting in this instance that Clawton Church Town is mentioned as early as 1088 when Judhael of Totnes, who held Clawton after the Conquest, made a gift of tithes 'in Clavatone near to Churcheton…' (Harvey 1939, 13). It would appear from this that the usage goes back to at least the 11th century.

Another example in North Devon is Instow where Instow Town with the barton and the church is up on the hill, while modern Instow is down by the main road, the old railway track and the sea. In the case of Instow, development by the seaside is probably relatively modern. Be that as it may, in all of the instances considered here, some factor has intervened to stimulate the reduction of the old manorial heart; the priorities that determined the heart of the settlement at the beginning - in some cases prominence, in other cases shelter from the elements, access to water and favourable land - have been superseded by agronomic or economic determinants of a different nature.

Somewhat different is the case of Arlington. As is evident from Nick Berry's contribution to this collection, Arlington has seen drastic changes to its landscape from

Plate 13.2:
The 17th century grave of John Allyn and his son Thomas of Clawton Church Town.
(Photo: T. Green.)

77

the partial conversion of a working estate in the late 18th century to the complete conversion into a pleasure park in the 19th century. The present Arlington house dates from 1820 when it was built on a new site. The exact location of the old, medieval and post-medieval Arlington House was for a long time lost to memory, but recently discovered 18th century plans make it evident that the house stood adjacent to the church. Documents of the 17th and 18th centuries refer to Arlington Town and Arlington Church Town as well as Arlington Barton; and within the park there remains a paddock called Town Meadow. Map evidence indicates that any farm or cottages that might have been located within Arlington Town were finally swept away between 1805 (OS Surveyor's Draft) and 1840 (tithe map). In this case therefore we are not dealing with settlement abandonment or shift, but with deliberate removal. The 'Town' element in the records and in the landscape serves in this case to confirm that before the status of Arlington was raised by Colonel Chichester around 1790, Arlington was a classic Devonshire rural settlement with church, barton and a number of tenements. There was even a 'bowling green', but that is another story to pursue.

So what is the significance of 'Towns' in the North Devon landscape? Principally, where the church and the 'Town' are now detached from the major settlement, it should be evident that the needs of settlement have changed, causing a shift or drift towards a different focus. The 'Town' is where the manor was first centred, and is or was represented by manor house and/or demesne farm or barton, church and probably a hamlet of cottages. The 'Town' is therefore where archaeological investigation might expect to find signs of early settlement, in many cases now abandoned and detectable only as 'humps and bumps'. Examples to consider are High Bray where Braytown is on the hill with barton, church and glebe, while Brayford is in the valley below, or Loxhore where North and South Town Farms are close to the church and where, as Nick Berry points out, substantial earthworks suggest a shrunken settlement. In the same area, Charles has its Town Barton adjacent to the church, again with some suggestion of a shrunken settlement in the nearby topography. Interesting too, in this case, is the evidence of a late prehistoric or Romano-British settlement immediately to the north of the barton and it is tempting to consider some sort of continuity.

Just to demonstrate with two examples that the 'Town' phenomenon is not restricted to North Devon, Doddiscombsleigh in South Devon has its Town Barton and church about half a kilometre from the existing village centre, while Luxborough in the Brendon Hills has Church Town on the hill, while the village lies in the valley below. And just to test the theory, a contrary example is provided by Bratton Fleming where Town Farm is at the southwest end of the village at some distance from the church.

In its scattered farms and hamlets and their attendant fields, as well as in the layout of its villages and small towns, the Devonshire landscape wears its history openly. An essential part of this historic fabric are the place-names which themselves carry important clues to the evolution of the pattern of dispersed settlement. Among these the Town Bartons and Church Towns might be dismissed as of little interest, while this brief study has attempted to suggest their potential importance in unravelling the processes of settlement evolution.

14
The Manor of South Hole, Hartland

Stephen Hobbs

The manor of South Hole was one of a small number of independent manors within the greater Hartland Hundred, the primary ones being Hartland and Stoke St Nectan. South Hole is a small valley landmass which borders the parish of Welcombe on the south and runs north along an un-named river valley to adjoin the tenements of Elmscott and Hardisworthy on the north and east and the Atlantic coast on the west.

Very little documentary evidence had been known to exist to illuminate the history of the manor. Recently, following the acquisition of the coastal fields by The National Trust, an archaeological report was prepared on the cliff top enclosure commonly known as Embury Beacon but there was little else. What is generally taken as South Hole history was as much as could be gleaned from the Domesday record and minor information available through the record of changing ownership. However the recent indexing of the document archive of Hartland Abbey has revealed an extensive sequence of manorial records of the Court Leete and Court Baron of South Hole. These are records previously unavailable for research. Within the archive are similar manorial records for Stoke St Nectan, Hartland, Harton Borough, Launcells, Pancrasweek, Week-St-Mary & Cookbury, again mostly previously inaccessible. The manor was sold to Paul Orchard of Hartland Abbey in 1715 by a Charles Snow for the sum of £160; the sale was accompanied by the transfer of the manorial documentation which in turn became part of the present Hartland Abbey Archive. The interesting exercise now is to link the new documentary evidence back to tenements and then to the land holdings of each such tenement.

Landscape study, by use of the Tithe Map, aerial photography and more recently satellite imagery, has shown the changing pattern of the field systems. Clearly evident on the Tithe Map, on the northern high ground of the manor, are the strip fields often associated with medieval farming. Modern farming has resulted in numerous amalgamations of such strips to produce the field pattern of today. However much of the ground is marginal and thus has not been made into such large fields, thereby losing the underlying features (Fig. 14.1). Further down the valley a range of small tenements clings to the steep hillside but does not show any perceptible field systems attached to any particular property. This may be determined by the terrain or may be indicative of an early system of enclosure.

Fig.14.1
Map of the manor
of South Hole.

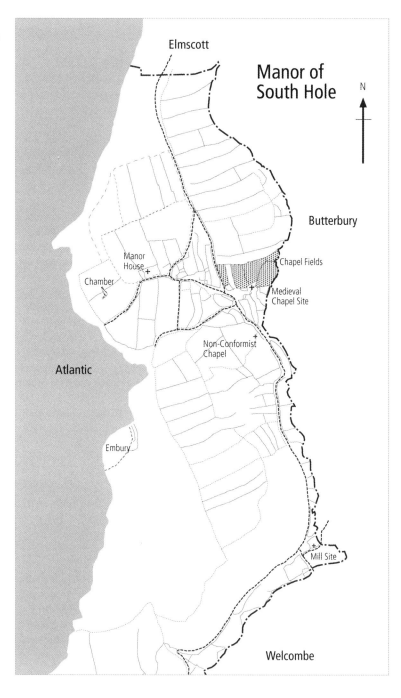

The old manor house was situated immediately to the west of the present South Hole Farm but no visible remains indicate its actual position. Field walking has produced a wide ranging collection of pottery finds along with some lithics. Some of the present buildings show evidence of building materials that have come from a substantial high status structure: Kings Cottage is a particularly good example. Whether these materials were from the old manor house or another building would be difficult to ascertain. An interesting event reported in the local press in the 1950s, concerned a farming accident: a tractor working in a field adjacent to South Hole Farm caused the collapse of the ground and exposed an underground structure. This was reported as being dry stone lined and over 50 foot in length. A small number of people visited and were able to enter the chamber before the exposed section was backfilled. A ground penetrating radar survey in 2007 has indicated the possible fuller extent of the chamber and leaves open the question of its purpose. It would appear to have an entry passage approaching from the west which turned north at a right angle to allow access into the main chamber. Suggestions range from a medieval storage chamber to souterrain, or, more romantically, a smuggler's cavern possibly associated with Cruel (Daniel Herbert) Copinger. Further research would be needed to establish the fuller extent and use of the chamber.

Plate 14.1 Gaming 'board' for the game of Nine Men's Morris scratched on a flat stone.

South Hole has an interesting religious history; it was the site of a chapel of St Heligan attached to the mother church of St Nectan. However, its actual location is not positively identified, and a small group of hillside fields, all with 'chapel' in their names and centred on the present holding called Kings Cottage, provide the only available clues. Recently a chance comment led to an invitation to visit the property to inspect a small length of foundation walling uncovered in one of the garden plots. In conversation with the property owner it transpired that during improvement to his house he had uncovered a number of interesting items, in particular a stone with a geometric pattern which he thought resembled Celtic or religious iconography (Plate 14.1). Inspection and confirmatory research has shown this to be an example of a 'board' game popular in the medieval period known as Nine Men's Morris. This particular artefact had been uncovered when an area of overgrown hillside was being prepared for use as a lawn and flower-beds. A tiled floor and associated cobbled path were revealed, and are now reburied. The 'stone' was lying on the tiled surface. Examples of this type of carving are rare with known examples scratched into the cloister seats of Canterbury, Gloucester, Norwich, Salisbury Cathedrals and Westminster Abbey (Bell, 1979) and on a pillar in Chester Cathedral (http://www.timetravel-britain.com/articles/churches/cathedral.shtml). That is not

to say it has any specific association with religious life, except possible light relief during long sermons, but may have been a workman's amusement. There is at present little contextual evidence to firmly date the stone or its surroundings although an invitation is extended for geophysics over portions of the property. (Instructions for playing the game and its modern derivatives are freely available on the Internet.)

Some may know South Hole as the birthplace of John Moreman, (c.1490) Roman Catholic priest. He matriculated from Oxford and was one time vicar of Midsomer Norton, 1516, and rector of Instow, 1522-36, then Holy Trinity, Exeter amongst others. However it was during his tenure as vicar at Menheniot, Cornwall that he was best known, his religious views at the time being controversial. He spent time confined in The Tower and was released on the accession of Queen Mary, 1542, and in 1554 she made him her chaplain. A fuller biography can be found at http://www.oxforddnb.com/view/article/19202

An early but short lived Non-Conformist chapel existed on a site just southwest of Kings Cottage. Little but the building platform remains, although there is a local suggestion that a small number of interments took place on the western perimeter of the chapel site. The seats from the chapel have been used as privacy infill to the seating in the south transept of St Nectan's Church, Stoke, where originally there were box-pews; some still bear the seat numbering (Plate 14.2).

On the southern edge of the manor at the junction of two rivers is Crenham Mill. This is a well documented mill, although the present domestic building is the result of rebuilding following a destructive fire in the 1970s. The mill itself is contained in an open fronted structure adjacent to the main entrance of the present dwelling house. The all wooden mechanism (Plate 14.3), although presently fragile, is sufficiently intact to allow a full recording which it is hoped will be undertaken shortly.

From this brief introductory article it can be seen that all the elements for an independent manor exist within this one small isolated valley. Further research, it is hoped, will be able to expand on the understanding of its makeup and operation.

15
A Fishery Dispute on the Taw

James Coulter

In his recently published book, *A Field Guide to the Archaeology of the Taw and Torridge Estuaries*, Chris Preece has suggested that in addition to being hunter-gatherers, our distant Mesolithic ancestors may also have been fishers. We don't actually know if they fished on the Taw for the earliest known record of this dates from the ninth century and somewhat later. When Lord Judhel founded the priory of St. Mary Magdalene in Barnstaple around 1170, he granted to it, among other emoluments, the tithes of the fishery at Tawstock. Further to these two early dates there exists a considerable body of evidence that fishing by means of weirs, traps or otherwise formed an important and lucrative part of the medieval economy with an apparent abundance of salmon and other species which present-day Taw fishermen can only dream about. The eighteenth century Dean Milles survey of Devon parishes records that trout, eel and salmon abounded in the Taw at all seasons. One salmon 4ft 9 inches long and weighing 57 pounds was sold at three halfpence a pound. In fact, salmon was so plentiful that farm workers would sometimes stipulate among their terms of employment that they should not be required to eat it on more than three days a week.

Records of disputes and legal wrangles over fishing rights give some idea of the lucrative nature of these fisheries. One such is the fourteenth century dispute between Walter Stapleton, Bishop of Exeter and William Martyn, lord of the manor of Tawstock. Without having obtained the necessary 'planning permission', Lord William built a watermill and proceeded to combine this with a fish-trapping construction in the Taw which abutted into the bishop's domain beyond the centre of the river at Bishops Tawton on the opposite side. It is instructive to note which of these two powerful magnates and landowners came off best when they took the matter to court, as detailed in the following abstract from an indenture held in the Devon Record Office, Exeter.

By reason of an abutment of a certain weir made at the land of Lord Walter de Stapleton, Bishop of Exeter in his manor of Bishops Tawton at the conduit of the mill of Lord William Martyn in his manor of Tawstock without the consent and volition of the Bishop, there was an occasion for a disagreement at Exeter on the Monday next after the feast of St Matthias the apostle (Feb. 24th) in the sixteenth year of the reign of King Edward II (1323).

William Martyn and his heirs to have and hold for ever the aforesaid abutment in form as follows. Namely, that before the feast of Michelmas next (29th September) the said William Martyn may make at his expense, two fish traps, which in the vernacular are called hattches to catch salmon and other fish (which) as often as needed he will improve, repair and maintain in good state continually at his expense for ever. And that the said Bishop of Exeter and his successors, free from all charge and expenses, may have half of the fish whithersoever in the said weir and in the bedum2 of the said mill and caught under it. And the bailiff of the Bishop of Exeter to have one close and the bailiff of William Martyn to have another close of these fish traps on condition that it is valid as impartial or mutual to take out or to have any fish. It is permitted to the bailiffs and servants of the said Bishop and William in the bedum and under the mill to take whatever fish it may please them without hindrance of multure3 of the said mill and that all fish taken there be divided equally between the aforesaid parties. And that all mills of the said William to be in the presentment of the Bishop of Exeter and by the corporal oath of God sworn and against this agreement he shall commit no contravention or infidelity in any part thereof. It will be permitted to the servants of the said Bishop and William the appointment of a watch of the said fish traps concerning the land from each pair of the water (closes) mill, bedum and under the mill to walk, sojourn and to return as much as it pleases them to watch the fish traps and to fish in the bedum of the mill and under it. And if the said servants by so walking, sojourning or returning in the corn or meadow cause loss or damage it (the agreement) is (to be) amended by another charge or claim.

If indeed it should happen that the abutment of the weir by force of the river, newly broken land or by any other means henceforth is broken or damaged, it is permitted to the aforesaid William that, as long as he observe this agreement in every part, to repair that weir and abutment as often as necessary and to ensure that by so doing a sufficient supply of water is diverted to the mill. And if it should happen, God forbid, that the aforesaid William should not observe this agreement in every part, then it is permitted to the Bishop to break the abutment and weir up to mid-stream of the Taw and appropriate to himself stones and other material from it and to dispose of these at will.

To which agreement in every part sworn, the aforesaid Bishop of Exeter firmly binds himself and his successors and the aforesaid William firmly binds himself and his heirs. In testimony for these writings indented and divided between the parties, the seals of the same by party, one with the seal of the Chapter of Exeter........are affixed. With these witnesses, Lord John of Carru, Richard of Merton, Nicholas of Bonevill, Richard of Stapeldon, Robert of Stokhaye, William Hereward, Roger the Jew, Knights and others. Given at Exeter the day and year written above.

It is worth noting that the agreement so reached includes only payments in kind between the parties and money payments are not mentioned. Although it was intended to last 'for ever', little did the parties know that, within a generation, their world would change for ever.

According to a fourteenth century chronicler: In the year 1348, in Melcombe, in the county of Dorset, a little before the feast of St John the Baptist, (24th June) two ships…came alongside. One of the sailors had brought with him from Gascony the seeds of the terrible *pestilence and, through him, the men of that town were the first in England to be infected'*(Ziegler 1997, 98) The 'terrible pestilence' was the great plague known colloquially as the Black Death, which in the preceding year had swept through continental Europe, and now spread quickly throughout the land killing at least a third and possibly as much as half the population of England. The resulting shortage of manpower brought about a crisis in the labour market and hastened the end of the centuries-old feudal landlord and tenant system in favour of a money based economy, as the reduced numbers of labouring peasants could now demand higher wages. No longer able to rely on the boon work of their tenants, it became more practical for landlords to lease (farm) their demesne ploughlands, mills, fisheries and suchlike in return for money rents—often to tenants or officials of the manor. Thus we find in the accounts of Geoffrey Moreland, Reeve to Lord John Bassett of the manor of Tawstock for the year 1396: *The rent of 16s. 8d for the farm of the fishery of the Taw demised to Oliver Rademan, bailiff for this year. And of 13d for the fishery of Bruggepol for this year.* The name 'Bruggepol' would seem to derive from the Old English *brycg* meaning bridge and *pol* – pool, suggesting the pool by the bridge which could mean either Newbridge or Longbridge, both of which were in existence in the fourteenth century.

Notes

1. DRO/W1258M/D1/6   (The author is indebted to Margaret Cameron for translation from the Latin).
2. bedum. Part of a millstream boarded up to increase the force of the water to turn the millwheel.
3. multure. A toll of grain or flour due to a miller for grinding corn.
4. Middleton MSS. Nottingham University. Department of Manuscripts.

Footnote: Evidently both mill and fishery were still in existence in 1773 as in the Tawstock rent roll for that year we find them paying an annual rent of £5. No known trace of either remains.

16
Celebrating Merton's Kingmaker

Tim Wormleighton

The year 2008 marked the 400th anniversary of the birth of George Monck, Duke of Albemarle and Earl of Torrington (Plate 16.1), one of the most influential characters of the English Civil War and Commonwealth period and a key player in the Restoration of the Monarchy, bringing much needed stability to the country. However, he is a figure who has been unfairly neglected in most popular accounts of British history. He was born at Great Potheridge in the parish of Merton, North Devon on 6th December 1608, the fourth child of Sir Thomas Monck, an impoverished landowner who had married the daughter of a wealthy Exeter merchant, Sir George Smyth. In view of his father's financial circumstances, the young George was brought up for a time by the Smyth family. Of his education, little is known, although one of his numerous biographers stated that he attended a local school in Devon.

At the age of 16 he entered upon what might be considered the obvious career choice for the younger son of impecunious gentry by joining a military expedition to Cadiz. He is known to have accompanied one of his Devon cousins, Sir Richard Grenville, who commanded a company of foot, although details of Monck's contribution to the campaign are sketchy. On his return to England he was involved in a notorious incident that resulted in him being accused of murdering an Exeter under-sheriff. The colourful story is recounted by Thomas Gumble, author of the first biography of Monck published just after his death, in 1672. It appears that Charles the First was visiting Plymouth in September 1625 to inspect his fleet moored there. All the local gentry, including Thomas Monck, were keen to see and be seen at this important royal event, but Thomas, as a debtor, was wary of being spotted and arrested by his creditors. To avoid this possibility, he sent his son, George, to present a substantial gift to the under-sheriff with a request that he might be able to attend the royal visit without fear of prosecution. The under-sheriff gave assurances that this would be the case, but on the day went back on his word and, as Gumble relates, *in a most treacherous manner seized the person of Sir Thomas Monck, upon an execution, in the face of the whole county, convened to receive his Majesty.* This outright humiliation to the Monck family in front of all the gentry of Devon was too much for the young George to bear and he sought out the under-sheriff responsible, delivering, according to Gumble, *due chastisement (as he well deserved) and had not some persons present interposed, had left him in a worse condition.* The details of the case were retold and elaborated by subsequent generations of Monck biographers but original documents preserved among the archives of the Exeter Quarter Sessions in the Devon Record Office reveal details of what actually took place. They show that George Monck was aided and abetted by his elder brother, Thomas, and John Pollard of Fowey, and that they sought out the under-sheriff, Nicholas Battyn of Stoke Canon, at the Bear Inn, South Street, Exeter. Monck allegedly assaulted him, chased him out of the inn and stabbed him as he lay on the ground so violently 'that his sworde turned almost double'. All three assailants were later arrested by the city authorities, although Monck's accomplices were released on bail. He was held in custody as it was feared that Battyn might die from his injuries. After a week or so it looked as if this was no longer a possibility and Monck was also given bail. However, Battyn succumbed sometime within the following three months and a warrant for the arrest of Monck for murder was duly issued in January 1627.

Plate 16.1
George Monck, Earl of Torrington.
(NDRO)

To avoid capture Monck absconded with another military expedition to France, where he distinguished himself in battle at the siege of La Rochelle. He was formally commissioned as an ensign in the company of foot of Sir John Burroughs, in which Sir Richard Grenville was serving as a captain. The death of Burroughs during this campaign provided an opportunity for promotion for both Devon men. When a second expedition to La Rochelle was dispatched in 1628, Grenville held the rank of colonel and Monck commanded his own company. However, as it turned out, the English army took no part in the action. After this campaign, Monck effectively disappears off the radar for the next three years, turning up again in 1631, serving as an ensign in the Earl of Oxford's foot regiment, as part of the Dutch forces fighting the Spanish in the Netherlands, notably at the siege of Maastricht in 1632, where the Earl was killed. In 1634 the new colonel, George Goring, appointed Monck to the rank of captain-lieutenant with command of its largest company of men. Monck became one of the heroes of the siege of Breda in 1637, leading the assault that led to the surrender of the town. Following this success, he resigned his commission over a dispute as to whether some of his men who were accused of misconduct should be tried by court martial or a civil court. He returned to England to sign up for the forces of King Charles the First against the Scottish covenanters, receiving the rank of lieutenant-colonel in the Earl of Newport's regiment of foot. He was the only officer to take any credit from the Scottish rout of the English at Newburn, protecting the ordnance during their retreat. He then turned his attention to the Irish rising in October 1641, securing the position of colonel in the 1,200 strong foot regiment of the Earl of Leicester, who was a relative. When he arrived in Ireland, Monck was also given the command of 2,500 men in the Earl of Ormond's force. He proved himself a brave and very competent leader during this time, so much so that Leicester proposed him for the position of governor of Dublin in 1642, although Charles insisted on the appointment of his own man.

On the outbreak of the English Civil War, Monck was among those officers who insisted, successfully, that the royal army in Ireland should take no oath of allegiance to either side in the conflict, but in September 1643, the end of the rebel uprising meant that the army was now free to return to England to fight for the king. Monck,

Plate 16.2
The house at Great
Potheridge.
(North Devon
Museums Trust)

however, maintained his refusal to swear allegiance to the king over Parliament and as a consequence was relieved of his command and sent as a prisoner to Bristol. However, Charles recognised that Monck's qualities were too valuable to be ignored and summoned him to a private meeting at Oxford, following which Monck was persuaded to command a new Royalist regiment of foot supplemented by those men returning from Ireland. He was captured soon after by a parliamentary force at the siege of Nantwich in January 1644 and imprisoned in the Tower of London. During this spell of imprisonment Monck wrote his own military manual, *Observations upon Military & Political Affairs*.

After the defeat of Charles the First and the Royalist cause, Monck readily professed an oath of loyalty to Cromwell and Parliament, and was appointed to military commands in Ireland and Scotland, attaining the rank of major-general on land and general-at-sea, making him one of the three joint commanders of the English fleet. In 1647, George's elder brother died and he inherited the family estate of Potheridge (Plate 16.2) in Merton, which was still heavily encumbered by debt. In January 1653 he married Anne Radford, the daughter of a London farrier, whose first marriage had ended in separation some years earlier. There was a hint of scandal about this union, as nobody knew whether Anne's first husband, Thomas Radford, was alive or dead, and Monck was marrying well beneath him. The evidence suggests that Anne had served as Monck's seamstress while he was imprisoned in the Tower.

After the death of Cromwell in 1658, Monck at first swore allegiance to his son, Richard, but when it became clear that Richard was an unsuitable successor, he entered into secret negotiations with Charles the Second's side, utilising his extensive network of Devon kinsmen, eventually paving the way for the Restoration of the Monarchy in 1660. When Charles landed at Dover to reclaim the throne, Monck was the first person to greet him. In reward for his loyalty, he was created Baron Monck of Potheridge, Earl of Torrington and Duke of Albemarle, with grants of land worth £7,000 per annum and an annual pension of £700. Among his new properties were a former royal palace, Theobalds, New Hall Estate in Essex, and the part of Whitehall known as The Cockpit for his London residence. His regiment of foot became the only part of Cromwell's New Model Army to be incorporated into Charles' military, becoming the Coldstream Guards, who maintain their link with Merton to this day. It is a measure of how highly the king thought of Monck that he was the first person Charles called upon to assist in the disasters of the Great Plague and the Fire of London in the mid 1660s.

It is thought that Monck made extensive improvements to his mansion at Great Potheridge in Merton from the Restoration to the time of his death. The impressive stable block, which still stands, was said to have sufficient room for 40 horses, perhaps in anticipation of a royal visit from his grateful sovereign.

Towards the end of his eventful life, Monck's physical health deteriorated noticeably. He became very swollen and short of breath, and he was unable to sleep lying down. He more or less retired from public life to spend his remaining days at his picturesque New Hall Estate. George Monck died at The Cockpit on the morning of 3 January 1670, the cause of death being recorded as dropsy. He received a state funeral at the King's own expense and a resting place of honour in Westminster Abbey. The funeral service was led by his sole surviving son, Christopher, and attended by the entire regiment of the Coldstream Guards.

The Lysons brothers report in their *Magna Britannia* of 1822 that *the title and the family became extinct in 1687 by the death of his only son, Christopher, Duke of Albemarle'* and that 'the manor of Potheridge now belongs to Lord Rolle, concluding that *the greater part of Potheridge House, which appears to have been finished in 1672, was pulled down after the Duchess's death, in 1734. The remainder has been fitted up as a farm-house. The chapel, which was of Grecian architecture, was in a ruinous state in 1770, and has since been taken down, except part of the western wall. The magnificent stables are still standing.* The gradual decline of Potheridge mirrored the fading reputation of Monck himself, who seems to have been increasingly overlooked as the national hero he undoubtedly was. Perhaps, in the long run, his capacity for effecting change in a calculating, behind the scenes manner, combined with his dogged ruthlessness, extreme political acumen and occasional brutality, are not qualities we naturally choose to associate with the more iconic figures from our history. As a correspondent to *The Times* aptly put it following a visit to the remains of Great Potheridge at the time of the national celebrations for George the Fifth's Silver Jubilee in 1935: *If some intelligent magnate of the films were to present the life history of this man to the public there would be a universal rustling of the leaves of history books. England has forgotten George Monck, but few Englishmen are less qualified for oblivion. "Stout and honest for his country", Pepys called him. This man was a great soldier, a great sailor, a great administrator, and a great man – one of the bravest, the simplest, and the best-loved of Englishmen. The story of his life is an incredible romance. The tale of what he endured, inspired, accomplished and attempted in 60 short years is an epic.*

This man established the British Regular Army and the Royal Marines.

This man was offered the Crown of England and refused it.

This man carried through, without shedding a drop of blood, a revolution that, beginning meanly, went on from strength to strength and came to full flower in the rejoicings on May 6 1935. On that day all England should have honoured him, but – his house is almost roofless and his name is almost forgotten.

Hopefully, the Monck 400 celebrations taking place in north Devon in the first decade of the twenty first century will do something to remind people of the enormous contribution of that great Devonian, General George Monck, to our national heritage and provide a lasting memorial to his achievements in the parish of his birth.

17
The Portable Antiquities Scheme (PAS) in North Devon.
Danielle Wootton

Introduction
This article lists all the items from the North Devon area which have been reported as potential Treasure since 1998. To date, a total of thirteen items have been reported in North Devon under the Treasure Act. Ten of these items have gone through the treasure process; their disposition is reported individually below. A further three items are currently going through the treasure process. Whilst these cases have not yet gone to inquest, it has been decided, for completeness, to include brief details in this article. Further details on these three items will be available in forthcoming Treasure Annual Reports (TAR) after the inquests have been held.

For items of potential treasure found within other areas of the county of Devon, please see the Treasure Annual Reports.

The definition of Treasure
Under the Treasure Act 1996, there is a legal obligation to report all finds of potential Treasure. The Treasure Act 1996 replaced the common law of Treasure Trove in England, Wales and Northern Ireland, and was extended on 1st January 2003. Full details of the Treasure Act 1996 can be obtained via the Department of Media, Culture and Sport (DCMS), from the Portable Antiquities Scheme, or locally via the Devon Finds Liaison Officer, based at the Royal Albert Memorial Museum in Exeter.

For information, a brief summary of what items are considered Treasure has been included here.

Items considered treasure:
- *Any item over three hundred years old and made of more than ten percent silver or gold.*
- *Two or more coins over three hundred years old, made of at least ten percent silver or gold and recovered from the same findspot.*
- *Ten or more coins over three hundred years old containing less than ten percent silver or gold recovered from the same findspot (e.g. ten or more copper alloy coins).*
- *Any group of two or more metallic objects of any composition of prehistoric date that come from the same findspot.*
- *Any object, whatever it is made of, that is part of the same find as another object of Treasure.*

- *Any other item that would have previously been Treasure Trove, but does not fall within the specific categories above. This category covers any objects which are under 300 years old, made substantially of silver or gold, that have been deliberately hidden with the intention of recovery, and whose owners or heirs are unknown.*

Reporting treasure

The penalty for not reporting treasure is imprisonment for up to three months and a fine of up to £5,000.

All finds of potential treasure must be reported to the Coroner for the District (in the instance of finds from the North Devon district, they must be reported to the Coroner for Exeter and Greater Devon). Potential treasure finds must be recorded within 14 days from the day the item was found, or within 14 days from the day that the find was realised to be potential treasure. The Devon Finds Liaison Officer is the main point of contact for treasure finds within the county, and can be contacted via the Royal Albert Memorial Museum, Exeter, or the Portable Antiquities Scheme head office at the British Museum.

Non- treasure finds

Whilst this article is concerned with items of treasure found in North Devon, it is important to note that all archaeological finds, not just treasure, are important in the study of archaeology. For example, finds of flint, worked bone and stone, pottery and non- precious metals can all provide extremely valuable information about how people lived in the past. To an archaeologist, it is just as important that a record with a findspot (or grid reference) is made of any non- treasure find. In cases of non- treasure, all items are returned to the finder after recording and photographing. Please contact the Devon Finds Liaison Officer if you have any finds to record or have identified.

List of items reported as potential Treasure from the North Devon area.

Pottington, Devon: **Post-medieval gold seal ring** DEV-8D2681
Date: 16th century **Finder**: Mr P Allaway **Date of discovery**: March 1998
Circumstances of discovery: While searching with a metal-detector.
Description: Gold seal ring, the bezel engraved with a heraldic family crest in the form of a tiger. Note: See Treasure Annual Report 1997–98, no. 95.
Disposition: Declared Treasure but North Devon Museums Service decided against acquiring the object.
D R M GAIMSTER , Pre- Construct Archaeology
(Reference: TAR 1998 – 1999, no 180: previously no. 95)

Putsborough, Devon: **Post-medieval silver finger ring** DEV-8D71A5
Silver ring with punched and engraved decoration (found in about 1997; on examination at British Museum found to be 19th century in date and thus not treasure; returned to finder).
J A RUDOE, British Museum, Department of Prehistory and Europe

(Reference: TAR 1998 – 1999, no 202)

Abbotsham, Devon: **9 gold coins of the 17th century and 425 silver coins of the 16th and 17th centuries** (PAS-BA48B2)

Deposited: Mid-1650s

Finders: Ms T Prouse and Mr T Fishleigh **Date of discovery**: 21 July 2001

Circumstances of discovery: During building activity.

Description: 9 gold coins of James I and Charles I and 425 silver coins of Edward VI to Commonwealth: England

Edward VI (2) Third Period: shilling, 1 (tun); sixpence, 1 (tun) Mary (1) Groat, 1 (pomegranate)

Philip and Mary (7) Shillings, 6 (Full titles 1554, 2; full titles undated, 1; English titles 1557, 1; English titles date illegible, 2); groat, 1 (lis)

Elizabeth I (186) Shillings, 30 (cross crosslet, 8; martlet, 3; A, 6; crescent, 1; hand, 1; tun, 3; woolpack, 4; key, 1; ?, REGI, 2; details illegible, 1); sixpences, 149 (pheon, 18; rose, 4; portcullis, 5; portcullis or lion, 1; lion, 3; lion or coronet, 1; coronet, 21; castle, 11; ermine, 12; acorn, 3; eglantine, 11; plain cross, 14; im illegible, 157–, 1; long cross, 2; sword, 2; bell, 2; A, 5; A or escallop, 1; escallop, 1; crescent, 1; hand, 6; tun, 9; woolpack, 1; key, 3; key or anchor, 1; anchor, 1; 1, 2; 2, 1; illegible, 5); milled sixpence, 1 (star); groats, 4 (cross crosslet); threepences, 2 (illegible)

James I (48) First coinage: shillings, 6 (thistle, 1; lis, 4; illegible, 1); sixpences, 5 (thistle, 3; lis, 2) Second coinage. Gold: unite, 1 (tun); halfcrowns, 2 (escallop, 1; cinquefoil, 1). Silver: shillings, 18 (lis, 4; rose, 6; escallop, 1; 4th bust im illegible, 3; key, 1; tun, 2; plain cross, 1); sixpences, 8 (lis, 1; rose, 1; lis or rose, 2; 3rd or 4th bust, 1; escallop, 2; coronet, 1) Third coinage. Gold: laurels, 2 (rose). Silver: shilling, 1 (lis); sixpences, 5 (rose, 2; thistle, 1; lis, 1; trefoil, 1)

Charles I (1625–49) (172)

Tower mint Gold: unite, 1 (heart); crowns, 3 (lis, 1; rose, 1; triangle-in-circle,1). Silver: half-crowns, 25 (bell, 1; tun, 1; triangle, 2; triangle-in-circle, 9; (P), 5; (P) or (R), 2; (R), 2; sun, 3); shillings, 111 (lis, 1; castle, 1; rose , 1; harp, 4; portcullis, 3; bell, 6; crown, 7; tun, 12; anchor, 6; triangle, 2; ?, N2229, 1; triangle, 6; star, 12; triangle-in-circle, 18; (P), 12; (R), 2; eye, 6; sun, 6; ?, N2231, 4; ?, 1); sixpences, 30 (rose, 1; harp, 1; ?, N2240, 1; bell, 2; tun, 6; ?, N2241, 2; tun, 1; anchor, 4; triangle, 1; group E, ?, 1; triangle, 1; triangle-in-circle, 4;

(P) or (R), 1; ?, N2246, 2; (R), 1; ?, N2247, 1)Other mints: Aberystwyth, half-crown, 1 (book); Bristol, shilling, 1 (B) Commonwealth (5)

Shillings, 5 (1651, 1; 1652, 1; 1653, 2; uncertain date, 1)

Ireland (10) James I: First Coinage: shillings, 6 (bell); Second Coinage: shilling, 1 (escallop); sixpences, 3 (martlet)

Spanish-American (2) Philip IV: 8-reales, 2 (Mexico, countermarked in Brazil 1643–52, 1; Potosi, 1)

Disposition: Bideford Museum

B J COOK, British Museum, Department of Coins and Medals

(Reference: TAR 2001 – 2002, no 214)

Landkey, Devon: **Post-medieval silver-gilt dress-hook** (2004 T425) (DEV-8DC1F3)

Date: 16th century **Finder**: Mr S Bracher **Date of discovery**: 2003

Circumstances of discovery: While searching with a metal-detector.

Description: A silver-gilt dress-hook with oval back-plate. The back-plate is decorated with a scalloped edge. The oval face is decorated with three filigree circlets each with a quatrefoil motif and central raised knop. Between are circles of filigree with three knops with a fourth large central one. There are traces of probable gilding in several areas on the surface. The attachment loop and hook are complete and soldered to the reverse, the angular loop being at right-angles to the back-plate.

Discussion: For similar examples see Treasure Annual Report 1998 – 1999, no. 210, and Treasure Annual Report 2001, no.148.

Disposition: Museum of Barnstaple and North Devon.

N POWELL, Formerly Devon Archaeological Finds Liaison Officer, Museum of London Archaeology Service

(Reference: TAR 2003 – 2004, no 263)

Plate 17.1: Post-medieval silver-gilt dress-hook found at Landkey

Tawstock, Devon: **Post-medieval silver buckle** (2004 T427) DEV-8DE6F1.

Date: Mid-17th or early 18th century

Finder: Mr S Bracher **Date of discovery**: July 2004

Circumstances of discovery: While searching with a metal-detector.

Description: Oval silver buckle, the tab bent over at the end. The reverse stamped with a maker's mark PA in a rectangular shield.

Discussion: This buckle is very close in form to a silver buckle found in Hampshire (Treasure Annual Report 2003, no. 229) which bore the mark of a local Winchester maker recorded by Kent (1992) enabling it to be dated as above. The PA mark on this buckle is not recorded by Kent and has not been identified, but there is no reason not to give it a similar date range.

Disposition: Museum of Barnstaple and North Devon.

J A RUDOE, British Museum, Department of Prehistory and Europe

(Reference: TAR 2003 – 2004, no 253)

Plate 17.2: Post-medieval silver buckle from Tawstock

Tawstock, Devon: **Post-medieval silver fork** (2004 T426) DEV-8E1F55

Date: About 1698 – 1700 **Finder**: Mr S Bracher **Date of discovery**: July 2004

Circumstances of discovery: Picked up from the surface of cultivated land.

Description: A silver dognose table fork with FW monogram; provincial, possibly a variation of an early mark of Edmond Richards, Exeter (ER in a shaped punch, struck three times). If so, the absence of Exeter assay marks which began in 1701, combined with the pattern would suggest the above date.

Discussion: There is a three-tine fork with dognose end and crest of the Russell family, marked three times on the stem with a maker's mark, provincial, about 1690, in Brown (2001), no.56b. The position of the initials for the owner shows which way up the fork was placed on the table, ie: opposite to 21st century practice. There is also a travelling cutlery set, London c. 1690 with dognose spoon and owner's initials in Goldsmiths' Company (1999), p.28, B174.

Plate 17.3: Post-medieval silver fork from Tawstock

Disposition: Museum of Barnstaple and North Devon.
J MADIN Curator, Royal Albert Memorial Museum
D THORNTON, British Museum, Department of Prehistory and Europe
(Reference: TAR 2003 – 2004, no 347)

Bishop's Tawton, Devon: **Postmedieval silver-gilt 'maidenhead' spoon finial** (2005 T210) DEV-5F3AA3
Date: 16th – 17th century.
Finder: Mr M Welsh **Date of discovery**: April 2005.
Circumstances of discovery: Whilst metal-detecting.
Disposition: Museum of Barnstaple & North Devon had hoped to acquire but withdrew, returned to finder.
N POWELL, Formerly Devon Archaeological Finds Liaison Officer, Museum of London Archaeology Service
(Reference: TAR 2005 – 2006, no 821)

Merton, Devon: **Postmedieval silver-gilt 'maidenhead' spoon finial** (2005 T63) PAS-8EA0B2
Date: 16th – 17th century
Finder: Mr S Maloney. **Date of Discovery**: October 2002.
Circumstances of discovery: Whilst metal detecting.
Disposition: Barnstaple & North Devon Museum had hoped to acquire but withdrew, returned to finder.
B McLEOD, British Museum, Department of Prehistory and Europe
(Reference: TAR 2005 – 2006, no 822)

South Molton, Devon: **Medieval silver huntsman's whistle** (2005 T22) DEV-BD3CF4
Date: 15th–16th century **Finder**: Mr R Bennett **Date of Discovery**: October 2002
Circumstances of discovery: Whilst metal detecting.
Plate 17.4: Medieval silver huntsman's whistle from South Molton

Description: A silver whistle cut from sheet and shaped into a tapering form. It has two applied transverse fillets at the widest end (the mouthpiece) and at the opposite end, which is damaged. At this point, there may have been a hollow cast sphere, with a 'pea' inside. An elaborate swag or garland of cast silver is soldered at three points and the whistle is surmounted by a punched Lombardic 'A'. Weight: 3.73g.
Discussion: A similar whistle is part of the collections of the Somerset County Museums. Several are in the collections of the Museum of London. Silver whistles were used by huntsman, also for signalling at sea and as badges of office. Those of base metal, such as tin or pewter, may have been used as souvenirs, like pilgrim badges.
Disposition: South Molton & District Museum, the landowner's share generously donated.
N POWELL, Formerly Devon Archaeological Finds Liaison Officer, Museum of London Archaeology Service
(Reference: TAR 2005 – 2006, no 564)

Tawstock, Devon: **Medieval silver-gilt iconographic finger-ring fragments** (2005 T208) DEV-5F02B4
Date: Late 15th–early 16th century **Finder:** Mr A.Shaddick **Date of Discovery:** 1998.
Circumstances of Discovery: Whilst metal detecting.
Description: Four fragments of a Medieval finger ring. The bezel consists of two grooved, vertical compartments which accommodate the engraved images of saints. In the left compartment is an image of St John the Baptist, holding his attribute of the Lamb of God and in the right is a female saint, possibly St Katharine. The hoop is almost entirely lost but a substantial part of the shoulders of the ring survives. On the left shoulder is a depiction of the Virgin and Child and on the right shoulder is a female saint, possibly St Barbara.
Disposition: Museum of Barnstaple & North Devon.
J P ROBINSON, British Museum, Department of Prehistory and Europe
(Reference: TAR 2005 – 2006, no 428)

Plate 17.5: Medieval silver-gilt iconographic finger-ring fragments from Tawstock

South Molton, Devon. **Medieval Gold finger ring** (2008 T731). DEV- 569EB4
Date: 12th or 13th century
Finder: Mr Phil Tonkins **Date of discovery:** 23rd October 2008
Circumstances of discovery: Whilst metal detecting.
Description: Gold medieval finger ring. The thin, plain wire hoop is circular in section. The hoop is now misshapen due to damage. The rectangular bezel, of which two of the sides remain, would originally have held a stone.
Discussion: This finger ring is comparable to one found in the Newark area of Nottinghamshire (2004 T472), and to a finger ring from Condover, Shropshire (2004 T495), both of which are recorded in the TAR 2004.
Dimensions: Weight: 1.78g; Diameter: 23mm
Due to its age and precious metal content, this object qualifies as Treasure under the stipulations of the Treasure Act 1996. NB This item is awaiting inquest. Disposition: still to be confirmed at time of publication:
Danielle Wootton, Devon Archaeological Finds Liaison Officer

South Molton, Devon. **Medieval Silver Huntsman's Whistle fragment** 2008 T710. DEV-8EB4A3
Date: 15th- 16th century
Finder: Mr P Tonkins. **Date of Discovery:** August 2008
Circumstances of discovery: Whilst metal detecting
Description: Silver hollow cast sphere from a huntsman's whistle. The pea is now missing. Decoration is applied on both sides in the form of a quatrefoil motif with a plain cross running through the centre.
Discussion: This fragment was found within very close proximity to the Silver Huntman's whistle found in October 2002 (see 2005 T22; TAR 2995 – 2006), and as such is most likely to be part of the same artefact.
NB this item is awaiting inquest.
Disposition: still to be confirmed at time of publication.
Danielle Wootton, Devon Archaeological Finds Liaison Officer.

18
Carbon 14 Dating: An Anniversary

James Coulter

As we celebrate the fiftieth anniversary of the founding of NDAS, it seems appropriate to mark the sixtieth anniversary this year of the discovery of carbon 14 (radiocarbon) dating which has made such a massive contribution towards establishing archaeology as a respected discipline with a credible scientific basis. We have seen in this collection the role that radiocarbon dating has played in the interpretation of prehistoric sites in North Devon.

The honour for this discovery must go to Willard F.Libby and his associates at the University of Chicago who first published the results of their research in 1949 for which Libby was awarded the Nobel Prize for Chemistry in 1960: Included in his citation were the words: *seldom has a single discovery in chemistry had such an impact on the thinking of so many fields of human endeavour. Seldom has a single discovery generated such wide public interest.*

Libby was able to demonstrate the reliability of radiocarbon dating by measuring the age of wood samples from the tomb of Egyptian Pharaoh Snefru (2613 – 2494BC) which could be independently dated from other sources as 2600BC. The same method of calibrating radiocarbon dates against materials of known date is still in use today.

Carbon is one of the oldest elements known to prehistoric Man as he raked the charcoal from the embers of his campfire and the charcoal often found in archaeological sites is still frequently the most easily datable material. The fourth most abundant element in the universe, carbon has the unique ability to combine with other elements to form literally millions of organic substances and in this regard is the basis of all known forms of life. In its commonest form its atomic structure is comparatively simple with a nucleus comprising six protons each having a positive electrical charge together with six neutrons with no charge and surrounded by a 'shell' of six electrons of equal but opposite charge to the protons orbiting planetary fashion around the nucleus so that the atom is electrically neutral and very stable (Fig 18.1).

(Carbon can actually exist in two other forms known as isotopes with seven or eight neutrons known as carbon 13 and 14 respectively). Both protons and neutrons have the same mass and together they constitute the atomic mass of the element (electrons are weightless) while the protons alone determine the atomic number (6) which is key in determining its characteristics and relationship to other elements. As

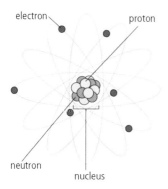

electron

proton

neutron

nucleus

example, the carbon nucleus with its six protons and six neutrons has an atomic mass of 12 with an atomic number of 6 usually written $^{12}_6C$ and known as carbon 12, the form in which it comprises some 99% of all carbon in the universe. Nitrogen, another element comprising 78% of the earth's atmosphere, has an atomic structure similar to carbon 12 but with one additional proton and in its most abundant form (nitrogen 14) one additional neutron giving it an atomic mass of 14 and an atomic number of 7 thus— $^{14}_7N$. Cosmic radiation consisting mainly of high energy protons originating deep in outer space bombards upper atmospheric gases producing a number of atomic particles including neutrons which are captured by nitrogen atoms transmuting them into carbon through the removal of one of their protons in a nuclear process which may be written:

Fig 18.1
The carbon 12 atom.

$$n + {}^{14}_7N \rightarrow {}^{14}_6C + p$$

where n represents a neutron and p is the proton removed from nitrogen to give the isotope carbon 14 which, unlike carbon 12 and 13 is unstable and subject to radioactive decay through which it reverts to nitrogen while emitting measurable subatomic *beta* particles which makes it so highly valuable in archaeological dating.

$$^{14}_6C \rightarrow {}^{14}_7N + e + Ve \quad (beta \text{ radiation})$$

Carbon 14 combines with atmospheric oxygen to form carbon dioxide (CO_2) which diffuses throughout the atmosphere at the very low concentration of one part per thousand billion ($1:10^{12}$) to become part of the so-called carbon cycle. Trees and other plants absorb atmospheric CO_2 and through the process of photosynthesis, convert it into wood and other plant tissues that are now 'labelled' with carbon 14 in approximately the same ratio to carbon 12 as they exist in the atmosphere. While the tree lives this ratio remains constant but when it dies and photosynthesis stops, the ratio of carbon 14 to carbon 12 begins to reduce as it decays. Thus, measuring how much carbon 14 remains in the dead wood provides a basis for determining when the tree died. Animals and humans ingest vegetation containing carbon 14 enabling their remains such as bones to be dated in a similar manner.

Radioactive isotopes decay at a rate whereby the number of radioactive atoms is always halved over the same fixed period of time which in the case of carbon 14 is 5730 years known as the half-life. After ten such half-lives, so little carbon 14 remains that it is virtually immeasurable, which limits it usefulness in dating to about 60,000 years. Within the context of archaeology in Devon, such a limitation need hardly concern us given that Cro-Magnon man, our nearest direct human ancestor, first enters the record in the Upper Palaeolithic, a mere 35,000 years ago.

Two different methods of analysis are commonly used in determining the age of archaeological materials—radiometric *beta* counting and Accelerator Mass Spectroscopy (AMS). The first, which has long been the traditional method, indirectly determines the amount of carbon14 present in the material examined by counting the number of radioactive *beta* decay emissions from it. The AMS technique, which has come into widespread use since the 1980s, directly measures the amount of carbon14 present by the use of an accelerator mass spectrometer, an instrument specifically designed to detect and separate extremely low concentrations of rare isotopes from an abundant isotope of the element. A sample to be analysed is reduced to either pure carbon or CO_2 and placed in an ionising chamber which, by the addition of one or more electrons to its 'shell', transforms the electrically neutral carbon atoms into negatively charged carbon ions and so rendering them susceptible to influence by electrical and magnetic forces. Formed into an ion beam comprising carbon12, 13 and 14 ions, this is accelerated through a sequence of strong electrical and magnetic fields which remove impurities and divides the three isotopes of carbon into separate beams before channelling them to different detectors where the ratio of carbon14 to the other two isotopes can be determined. One of the great advantages of the AMS technique over radiometric *beta* counting is that it can be used with samples as small as 100 micrograms of final carbon which is why it is so eminently suitable for analysing such rare artefacts as the Turin Shroud or the Dead Sea Scrolls. Radiometric analysis on the other hand requires samples containing 2 to 4 grams of final carbon but is generally less costly than the AMS method. The two methods have similar accuracy for optimally sized samples but AMS does tend to have the edge on sensitivity and precision.

Writing in 1979 Desmond Clarke expressed the view: *were it not for radiocarbon dating, we would still be floundering in a sea of imprecisions sometimes bred of inspired guesswork but more often of imaginative speculation.*

I am indebted to Professor Gordon Cook of Scottish Universities Environmental Research Centre for correcting the text and offering many helpful suggestions for improving it. Any remaining deficiencies are mine alone. JC

Bibliography and References

5 A Bronze Age Settlement at Holworthy Farm, Parracombe

Nowakowski, J.A. 1991. Trethellan Farm, Newquay: the Excavation of a Lowland Bronze Age settlement and Iron Age Cemetery, *Cornish Archaeology* 30, 5-242.
2001: Leaving Home in the Cornish Bronze Age: Insights into Planned Abandonment Processes, in Bruck, J.(ed.) *Bronze Age Landscapes: Tradition and Transformation, Oxford.*
Riley, H. and Wilson-North, R. 2001: *The Field Archaeology of Exmoor*, English Heritage.
Todd, M. 1998: A Hillslope Enclosure at Rudge, Morchard Bishop, in *Proceedings of the Devon Archaeological Society*, Vol.56, 133-152.

6 An Iron Age roundhouse at Middle Burrow Farm, East Worlington

Ghey, E., Edwards, N., Johnston, R. and Pope, R. 2007: 'Characterising the Welsh Roundhouse: Chronology, inhabitation and landscape' *Internet Archaeology* 23.
Pope, R. 2008: 'Roundhouses – 3000 years of prehistoric design' *Current Archaeology* 222, 14-21.
Reynolds, P. J. 1993: 'Experimental Reconstruction' in *An Iron Age Settlement in Dorset: excavation and reconstruction.* Edinburgh University

7 Ancient Hoofprints at Northam Burrows

Pasmore, A.J. 2009: *Archaeological Recording at Northam Burrows, Northam, Devon.* Exeter Archaeology Report No. 09/70.

8 Mines, Mills and Monasteries: A volunteer's account of digging at Combe Martin

Claughton, P. 2003: *Silver Mining in England and Wales 1066 to 1500*, Volume 1, 110: unpublished PhD Thesis, Exeter University
Godwin, H, 1967: The Ancient Cultivation of Hemp, *Antiquity* 41, 42-8 and 137.
North Devon Record Office: B9/5/31
The pottery sherds were identified by John Allen of the RAM Museum Exeter.

9 The Past, Present and Future of Palaeoenvironmental Research in North Devon

Balaam et al 1987: *Studies in Palaeoeconomy and Environment in South West England*, Oxford BAR British Series181.

Caulfield, S 1978: Neolithic fields: the Irish evidence, in: Bowen, H.C. and Fowler, J.C. (eds) *Early Land Allotment*, Oxford BAR British Series, 137-144.

Francis, P.D. and Slater, D.S. 1990: A record of vegetation and land use change from upland peat deposits on Exmoor, Part 2: Hoar Moor *Somerset Archaeology and Natural History Society Proceedings* 134, 1-25

Francis, P.D. and Slater, D.S. 1992: A record of vegetation and land use change from upland peat deposits on Exmoor, Part 3: Codsend Moor *Somerset Archaeology and Natural History Society Proceedings* 136, 9-28

Fyfe, R.M. 2000: *Palaeochannels of the Exe catchment: their age and an assessment of their archaeological and palaeoenvironmental potential* Unpublished PhD Thesis, University of Exeter

Fyfe, R.M. 2006: Sustainable conservation and management of the historic environment record in upland peat: a view from Exmoor, *International Journal of Biodiversity Science and Management 2*, 146-149.

Fyfe, R.M. (in review) The pattern of vegetation development on Exmoor. *Proceedings of the Somerset Archaeology and Natural History Society.*

Fyfe, R.M., Brown, A.G. and Coles, B.J. 2003a: Mesolithic to Bronze Age vegetation change and human activity in the Exe Valley, Devon, UK, *Proceedings of the Prehistoric Society 69*, 161-181

Fyfe, R.M., Brown, A.G. and Rippon, S.J. 2003b: Mid- to late- Holocene vegetation history of Greater Exmoor, UK: estimating the spatial extent of human-induced vegetation change, *Vegetation History and Archaeobotany* 12, 215-232

Fyfe, R.M., Brown, A.G. and Rippon, S.J. 2004: Characterising the late prehistoric, "Romano-British" and medieval landscape, and dating the emergence of a regionally distinct agricultural system in South West Britain. *Journal of Archaeological Science* 31, 1699-1714.

Fyfe, R.M. and Greeves, T. (in prep.): A new stone row on Dartmoor: chronology and landscape, *Proceedings of the Prehistoric Society*.

Merryfield, D.L. 1977: *Palynological and stratigraphical studies on Exmoor* Unpublished PhD Thesis, Kings College London

Merryfield, D.L. and Moore, P.D. 1974: Prehistoric human activity and blanket peat initition on Exmoor, *Nature* 250, 439-441

Riley, H. and Wilson-North, R. 2001: *The Field Archaeology of Exmoor*, English Heritage, Swindon

Rippon, S.J., Fyfe, R.M. and Brown, A.G. 2006: Beyond villages and open fields: the origins and development of a historic landscape characterised by dispersed settlement in South West England, *Medieval Archaeology* 50, 31-70.

10 Badges of Self-Esteem; An Assessment of Bottle Seals from North Devon

Unpublished sources

Account roll of Arundell family of Lanherne and Trerice, dated 1393-94 (Cornwall Record Office AR/2/539/5).

Extracts from letters of Lt. Col. E.H. Sweet 1964 (South Molton Museum).

South West Archaeology 2005 'Berry House Farm, Hartland, Devon; Results of an Archaeological Desk-based Assessment and Survey of Buildings' (S.W.Arch. report 050622).

South West Archaeology 2006 'The Stables, Youlston Park, Shirwell, Devon. Results of an Archaeological Watching Brief' (S.W.Arch. report 060105).

Published sources

Alexander, J. and Hooper, W. 1948: *The History of Great Torrington in the County of Devon*, Norwich.

Blanchard, L. (ed.) 1990: *Archaeology in Barnstaple 1984-90*, North Devon District Council.

Chope, R. 1940: *The Book of Hartland*, Torquay

Colby, F. 1872: *The Visitation of the County of Devon 1620*, London.

Coulter, J. 1996: *Tawstock and the Lords of Barnstaple*, Bideford.

Drake, Sir W. 1886: *Devonshire Notes and Notelets principally Genealogical and Heraldic*, London.

Dumbrell, R. 1983: *Understanding antique wine bottles*, Antique Collector's Club.

Duffy, M., Fisher, S., Greenhill, B., Starkey, D. and Youings, J. (eds) 1992: *The New Maritime History of Devon Vol. 1. From Early Times to the Late Eighteenth Century*, London.

Fisher, S. 1992: Devon's Maritime Trade and Shipping 1680-1780, in Duffy et al. (eds.). *The New Maritime History of Devon Vol. 1*, London, 232-241.

Fox Davies, A 1929: *Armorial Families: a Directory of Gentlemen of Coat-Armou*, London.

Hobbs, S. 2005: St. Nectan's: *A Question of a Seat*, Hartland Digital Archive.

Hoskins, W.G. 1954 *Devon*, London.

Langford, P. 1988: The Eighteenth Century, in Morgan, K (ed.) *The Oxford History of Britain*, Oxford.

Leeson Day, W. I. 1934: *Holsworthy; Devonshire Association Parochial Histories of Devonshire* No. 2, Torquay.

Melhuish, G. 1991: *Ashwater Church and Parish: Some Historical Notes* (Ashwater).

Morgan, R. 1977: *Sealed bottles: their history and evolution*, Midlands Antique Bottle Publishers.

Oliver, S. 2002: *Introduction to Heraldry*, London.

Pigot, J. (ed) 1830: *Pigot and Co.'s National Commercial Directory*, London and Manchester.

Rogers, W. 1942: Barnstaple Turnpikes Trust, *Transactions of the Devonshire Association*. 74, 139-167.

Rowe, J. 1994: *The North Devon Yeomanry 1794 -1924*, N. Devon Museums Service.

Ruggles-Brice, S. 1949: *Sealed Bottles*, London.

Tuckett, J. C. 1860: *Devonshire Pedigrees*, London.

Vivian, J. 1895: *The Visitations of the County of Devon*, Exeter.

Wills, G. 1974 *English Glass Bottles 1650-1950 for the Collector*, Edinburgh.

Youings, J. and Cornforth, P. 1992: Seafaring and Maritime Trade in Sixteenth-Century Devon, in Duffy et al (eds.) *The New Maritime History of Devon Vol 1*, London, 98-107.

11 Arlington Court, Devon

Cornforth, J. 1981: Arlington Court, Devon. *Country Life,* 169, 30th April 1981: 1178-1181.
Fox, A. 1955: Twenty-second report on the archaeology and early history of Devon. *Transactions of the Devonshire Association* 87: 319-320.
Humphreys, C.C. 1996: *Arlington, the Pond in the Wilderness,* National Trust.
Humphreys, C.C. 1999 and 2007: *Survey of the Wilderness and report on the excavation of the pond,* National Trust
Humphreys, C.C. and Green, T. 1998: *Excavation of a drain, south of the church at Arlington,* National Trust.
The National Trust 1985: *Arlington Court,* National Trust Guidebook.
Reichel, Rev. O.J. 1935: The Hundreds of Devon. Part VIII. The Hundreds of Braunton, Shirwell and Fremington, *Transactions of the Devonshire Association* Extra Vol. 387-495.
Victoria County History 1906: *History of Devonshire.* Vol. 1. London.

13 Going to Town

Harvey, H.H. 1939: *History of Clawton,* London.
Lysons, D & Lysons S. 1822: *Magna Britannia,* Vol. 6, London.
Morris, R. 1989: *Churches in the Landscape,* London.
Smith, A.H. 1970: *The Place-Name Elements* (Part 2), Cambridge.
Thorn, C. & Thorn, F. 1985: *Domesday Book: Devon,* Chichester.

14 The Manor of South Hole, Hartland

Bell, R.C. 1979: *Board and Table Games from Many Civilizations,* Volume 1, Oxford.

15 A Fishery Dispute on the Taw

Preece, C. 2008: *A Field Guide to the Archaeology of the Taw and Torridge Estuaries,* Bideford.
Ziegler, P. 1997: *The Black Death.* London.

17 The Portable Antiquities Scheme (PAS) in North Devon

Treasure Annual Report 1997 – 1998, Department Culture Media and Sport
Treasure Annual Report 1998 – 1999, Department Culture Media and Sport
Treasure Annual Report 1999 – 2000, Department Culture Media and Sport
Treasure Annual Report 2000- 2001, Department Culture Media and Sport
Treasure Annual Report 2001- 2002, Department Culture Media and Sport
Treasure Annual Report 2002- 2003, Department Culture Media and Sport
Treasure Annual Report 2003- 2004, Department Culture Media and Sport
Treasure Annual Report 2004- 2005, Department Culture Media and Sport
Treasure Annual Report 2005 – 2006, Department Culture Media and Sport
The Treasure Act 1996, Department of Culture Media and Sport
Advice for Finders of Archaeological Objects, Including Treasure (leaflet), Portable Antiquities Scheme